CONVERSATIONS WITH FAMILIES OF CHILDREN WITH DISABILITIES

Conversations with Families of Children with Disabilities creates a space for diverse families of children with disabilities to share their stories with pre-service and in-service teachers. Specifically designed for professionals preparing to work with families of children with disabilities, this text invites the reader to listen in as families reflect on their personal journeys in conversation with the authors. This powerful book helps educators develop a deeper understanding of families and enhance their capacity for authentic partnerships.

Victoria I. Puig is Associate Professor in the Department of Teaching and Learning and the Ben Samuels Children's Center Faculty Liaison at Montclair State University, USA.

Susan L. Recchia is Professor Emeritus of Early Childhood and Special Education and former Faculty Director of the Rita Gold Early Childhood Center at Teachers College, Columbia University, USA.

CONVERSATIONS WITH FAMILIES OF CHILDREN WITH DISABILITIES

Insights for Teacher Understanding

Victoria I. Puig and Susan L. Recchia

Routledge
Taylor & Francis Group

NEW YORK AND LONDON

First published 2021
by Routledge
52 Vanderbilt Avenue, New York, NY 10017

and by Routledge
2 Park Square, Milton Park, Abingdon, Oxon OX14 4RN

Routledge is an imprint of the Taylor & Francis Group, an informa business

Library of Congress Cataloging-in-Publication Data
Names: Puig, Victoria, author. | Recchia, Susan, author.
Title: Conversations with families of children with disabilities :
insights for teacher understanding / Victoria Puig and Susan L. Recchia.
Identifiers: LCCN 2020019306 (print) | LCCN 2020019307 (ebook) |
ISBN 9781138310919 (hardback) | ISBN 9781138310940 (paperback) |
ISBN 9780429459153 (ebook)
Subjects: LCSH: Special education--Parent participation. |
Special education--Psychological aspects. |
Special education teachers--Training of. | Parent-teacher relationships.
Classification: LCC LC3969 .P797 2020 (print) |
LCC LC3969 (ebook) | DDC 371.9--dc23
LC record available at https://lccn.loc.gov/2020019306
LC ebook record available at https://lccn.loc.gov/2020019307

ISBN: 978-1-138-31091-9 (hbk)
ISBN: 978-1-138-31094-0 (pbk)
ISBN: 978-0-429-45915-3 (ebk)

Typeset in Bembo
by Taylor & Francis Books

CONTENTS

ACKNOWLEDGEMENTS

We would like to express our deepest appreciation to the families who are the heart and soul of this book. They inspire us with their passion, their tireless work, and, most of all, their love. We celebrate their amazing determination in advocating for their children, their willingness to engage in the process of educating others, and their courage to share their stories.

1

INTRODUCTION

Conversations with Families offers a platform for families of children with disabilities to share their stories in their own words. Conceived as a supplemental text to be used in courses that focus on preparing professionals to work in partnership with families, this book invites the reader to listen in as families reflect on their personal journeys in conversation with the authors. In our role as liaisons between the families and developing professionals, we offer questions after each story to guide discussion.

Drawing on our shared experiences in the field as practitioners and teacher educators, we recognize that partnerships that value family strengths and resources are foundational for responsive teaching and learning. Throughout the interview process and the creation of the book, our stance toward families is one of support and acceptance, creating a safe space that invites authentic sharing and is open to hearing their stories as they are told. Our goal for this book is to bring greater awareness to the importance of listening to families and learning from their individual perspectives.

Background

Families of children with disabilities have historically been described using a "tragedy metaphor" (Maul & Singer, 2009, p. 155), in which negative outcomes and experiences were viewed as inevitable and normative for parents, siblings, and even extended family members. These assumptions guided research that focused on pathology, and positioned families as victims. Failing marriages, sibling anxieties, and extensive family stress were emphasized as expected responses to their challenges, without considering family strengths and resources as a catalyst for resilience. This focus on pathology and stress in families has also influenced professionals' perspectives and guidelines for intervention. Parents have been labeled "in denial" when they are too hopeful for their children's potential success or disagree with a professional's assessment or recommendations, and professional protocols for intervention can inadvertently undermine families' own strategies for teaching and caring for their children, calling into question their efficacy and commitment (Gallagher, Fialka, Rhodes, & Arceneaux, 2002; Goodley & Tregaskis, 2006).

Questioning the power and influence of this pathological perspective, some researchers have looked beyond this framework to uncover the strengths and resources that families bring to the challenges presented by disability (Maul & Singer, 2009; Puig, 2012). Looking through the lens of family resilience allows for greater understanding of families' adaptability (Lee, Park, & Recchia, 2016; Patterson, 2002). Findings from studies that apply resiliency theory, a strengths-based approach, show that most families of children with disabilities are resilient in similar ways to other families (Singer, 2006). Components of resilience such as family connectedness and closeness, the ability to make meaning of their circumstances, and spiritual and personal growth through the process of being and growing together, contribute to family well-being and stability (Bayat, 2007).

Gallimore and his colleagues (Gallimore, Goldenberg, & Weisner, 1993; Gallimore, Weisner, Kaufman, & Bernheimer, 1989) developed a research paradigm using eco-cultural theory as a framework for studying everyday life in families of children with disabilities. They explored how families actively constructed their own eco-cultural niches, developing routines that made sense for them in response to adverse circumstances. Families in their studies proactively made accommodations for their children with disabilities, demonstrating their resourcefulness in creating greater family harmony using their own strategies.

Applying this theoretical frame, Maul and Singer (2009) discovered that families of children with disabilities were not only resourceful and creative in finding adaptations that worked for them, but also, contrary to the tragedy metaphor, they often worked together as a team to care for their children or siblings with disabilities. Although sometimes faced with unique challenges, these families took action to negotiate them. The strategies that families developed emerged from and reflected their values, beliefs, cultural understandings, determination, and resourcefulness. Interestingly, scholarly findings have also revealed that when family preferences and values are used to guide interventions, as opposed to applying more prescriptive, standardized methods, interventions are more likely to be sustained over time (Moes & Frea, 2000).

Despite growing social awareness about the rights of people with disabilities, families continue to be challenged by negative public perceptions and responses to disability in their communities (Goddard, Lehr, & Lapadat, 2000; Goodley & Tregaskis, 2006). Judgments from others and lack of support from professionals to help navigate community experiences have been viewed as key stressors for families, especially when their children's disabilities include challenging behavior (Ludlow, Skelly, & Rohleder, 2012). Families have unique insights into their children's preferences and interests, and are "the sole owners of knowledge about their own family systems" (Dunlap & Fox, 2007, p. 276). Listening to families with an openness to thinking together about intervention strategies that fit the context of their lives can guide professionals to work more effectively to meet children's and families' needs.

Working with families has been a topic of considerable research and is an integral element of teacher education and professional development. However, many current publications such as traditional text books and collections of case studies are presented from a professional perspective. This book is unique in that it features a collection of diverse families' lived experiences shared in their own voices, and positions family stories at its heart. The authors' ongoing relationships with the families foster less formal and more candid conversations that transcend the constraints of traditional professional protocols. As liaisons, we draw on our professional expertise as well as our pre-existing relationships with the families to access their unique strengths and perspectives, and make connections between their experiences and professional practices and guidelines.

What Brought us to this Project?

We come to this project with a deep respect for children with disabilities and their families. Our experiences as special education teachers in various contexts inform our beliefs about the critical importance of understanding families' perspectives as a component of making meaningful connections with children that lead to optimal educational outcomes (Bayat, 2007). We have learned that every family has a story, and through telling their stories, they share the essence of who they are and what matters most to them (Goddard et al., 2000).

Through our work as teacher educators, we have witnessed the ways that students and teachers alike can lose sight of family perspectives in their eagerness to meet their own expectations for children or those of a standardized protocol (Prezant & Marshak, 2006). This has fueled our desire to make families' stories accessible to teacher educators and their students (Blue-Banning, Summers, Frankland, Nelson, & Beegle, 2004), as the beauty of family strength and resilience is often lost in prescriptive understandings of families' experiences and institutional needs (Goodley & Tregaskis, 2006; Maul & Singer, 2009). Learning about what families see as helpful supports for their own lives and the lives of their loved ones can help practitioners to look beyond a one-size-fits-all set of recommended intervention strategies and to challenge existing assumptions about what is considered "best practice" (Prezant & Marshak, 2006).

Our Interview Process

Various aspects of our work have brought us into contact with families of children with disabilities. In our more current roles as teacher educators, both authors have been affiliated with university-based inclusive child care centers and have invited parents and family members to be guest speakers in our courses. Through these practices, we have had the opportunity to get to know families over time. In conceptualizing *Conversations with Families*, our goal was to invite a diverse cross-section of families as participants, and to engage them in the process of telling their own unique stories. We were interested in learning more about their experiences as a family, as well as their thoughts and feelings about their interactions with professionals.

Participants were given the option to provide pseudonyms for each family member unless, like some, they preferred to use their own names. They were also given the opportunity to review transcripts and completed chapters. In order to maintain a sense of continuity throughout the story chapters, we designed a series of open-ended questions that were used flexibly to guide our conversations.

The interview protocol consisted of five overarching questions/invitations:

1. Tell me about your family.
2. Tell me about your child.
3. Tell me about your child/ren's educational experiences.
4. Tell me about your family's daily life and community experiences.
5. What advice do you see as most helpful to others?

Within each of these categories were sub-questions which were used as needed to expand or clarify responses. The full interview protocol can be found in the Appendix.

We each invited individual families that we had worked with previously to participate. In most cases, an initial e-mail was sent to the family with a very brief description of the book project and a request regarding their interest. Once interest in the project was confirmed, a more detailed description of what would be involved was shared. Interviews were scheduled in accordance with family preferences for time and place. Our conversations took place in an academic office, at the family's home, or in a local café, depending on what worked best for the families. Some conversations took place with just one parent, while others included whole families. During our time together, the interview protocol was used as a guide to support families to share their stories in their own words. Interviews were audio recorded and later transcribed. A copy of the transcript was shared with the family to check for accuracy, and to allow them to make any additions or deletions.

Descriptions of the Families

In our quest to represent a range of family structures, styles, and roles, we invited six families to participate. The children ranged in age from 4 to 16 years, and their disabilities included autism, Usher Syndrome, cerebral palsy, and schizencephaly, a rare neurological disorder. Families represent multiple ethnicities, cultures, and social classes. Each family and each conversation is unique. The children's needs and levels of independence also vary greatly, so that taken together, the family stories give access to a wide range of complexities involved across and within different disabilities.

Because we had previous relationships with our participating families, our interview conversations often touched on our shared history. Knowing more about what took place for the children and families in the years preceding these interviews brought a richer context to the discussions and allowed the conversations to flow more easily. In some cases, the interview transcripts were enhanced by information from other sources, described within the context of the chapters.

Essence of the Stories

After each family conversation was recorded and transcribed, we engaged in the process of crafting the family's story. Influenced by the work of Lawrence-Lightfoot and Davis (1997), we attempted to compose each story through a lens of "goodness" (Lawrence-Lightfoot, 2016, p. 20), focusing on family strengths in light of their lived realities. Although the conversations were framed in part by the interview questions, each took on a life of its own in process. In transforming the interview transcripts into families' stories, we worked to preserve their wholeness and integrity, weaving their words throughout. Although greatly informed by the conversations, the chapters were written by the authors, who ultimately influenced the way each story is shared with the reader.

Each family conversation is contained within its own chapter. We chose to present each family's story as a whole, without the interruption of scholarly interpretation or confirmation. Instead, we provide a set of questions for the reader at the end of each chapter along with relevant connections to the literature in the first and final chapters of the book.

Brief Description of the Chapters to Follow

Following this introductory chapter, six family story chapters each feature a conversation between one of the authors and a family. These exchanges are guided by families' unique experiences and priorities and their beliefs about what they would like professionals to know and understand about working with children with disabilities and their families. The interview questions and sub-questions encouraged them to identify their families' strengths, consider particular experiences and decisions that have shaped their children's and families' lives, and express their hopes for the future. More specific descriptions for each chapter's content are offered below.

Chapter 2: A Mother and Grandmother Come Together as Caregivers

In this chapter, we meet a mother and grandmother of an adolescent with multiple disabilities as they reconnect with one of the authors. Together they reflect on a conversation that was inspired by an assignment completed when the mother was the author's student in a class on building partnerships with families of children with disabilities. In telling their story, they trace their experiences, reflect on their feelings, and discuss their shared roles as caregivers.

Chapter 3: A Mother Learns to Advocate for a Preschooler with Complex Needs

This chapter reconnects one of the authors with the mother of a young child, labeled on the autism spectrum, who has transitioned from an inclusive child care setting to a self-contained special education classroom. The conversation uncovers the complexities of understanding her child's needs and advocating for an optimal educational environment and comprehensive supports. We intersect with this family at a time when they are still coming to terms with their different understandings of their child's diagnosis and their visions for his future.

Chapter 4: A Family Reflects on the Challenges and Achievements in their Daily Lives

This chapter introduces a family with two elementary-aged children on the autism spectrum and their young adult sibling. The conversation includes both parents and one of the authors. Discussion points highlight how this family navigates their daily experiences and evolving life transitions, negotiates their roles and responsibilities, and capitalizes on their unique blend of strengths and resiliencies.

Chapter 5: A Mother Reclaims her Strength and Confidence Negotiating the Complexities of Schooling for her Child

In this chapter one of the authors reconnects with an immigrant family who struggles to find an appropriate educational setting for their son with disabilities. The conversation brings to light the unique challenges that families encounter when their child's disability is difficult to diagnose and address. This family's resilience and resourcefulness in adapting to changes in their life are woven throughout our discussion.

Chapter 6: Parents Collaborate to Support their Sons' Health and Educational Achievement

In this chapter the author talks with the parents of two sons, one with cerebral palsy, and the other diagnosed on the autism spectrum. The conversation focuses on the boys' diverse capabilities and needs and how these parents work together to navigate medical services and educational systems for their sons. They speak candidly about their relationships with professionals and the ways they seek out and create inclusive educational and community experiences for their family.

Chapter 7: A Family Reflects on their Achievements and Dreams

This chapter introduces a family with two teenage sons with Usher Syndrome, a genetic disease that causes hearing loss, vision loss, and difficulties with balance. It presents a conversation between the young men and their parents during which they reflect on their experiences and achievements, consider their relationships with professionals and other support systems, and articulate their life philosophies and goals for the future. Their strong family bond and determination are recognized as key assets.

Chapter 8: An Unexpected Reciprocity: Guest Speakers Learn by Sharing their Stories

One additional chapter has been included which is distinct from the others in that it describes the ways that individuals with disabilities, professionals, and families of children with disabilities were integrated into one of the authors' courses on partnerships with families. It also describes a project specifically designed to access a diverse group of guest speakers' insights into their experience. While their inclusion in the course was intended to enhance the students' learning, an unexpected reciprocity was revealed when these individuals shared how they valued the experience. We include this chapter as a way of emphasizing the power of telling one's story, which we believe resonates throughout the book.

Chapter 9: Concluding Thoughts

This final chapter presents a summary of the themes that run through each of the families' stories. It highlights the impressive array of family strengths and resources that emerge as families work to meet their unique challenges. We share families' advice for working together, advocating for their children, and building reciprocal partnerships with professionals. In this final chapter, we discuss the ways that these family stories resonate with research from the field and present enduring lessons for teacher educators, teacher education students, and practitioners to continue to ponder.

How Stories Contribute to the Process of Teacher Education

Taken together, the chapters of this book offer a rich tapestry of the thoughts and feelings of diverse families of children with disabilities. They represent families' unique experiences and priorities, and their beliefs about what they would like professionals and other people to know and understand. Participants identify their family strengths, consider particular experiences and decisions that have shaped their children's and families' lives, and express their hopes for the future. Readers have the opportunity to learn from the powerful stories that families tell and to better understand the ways that diverse circumstances can afford possibilities and uncover family capacities. In speaking about life stories, Beck (2015) describes them as not only a way to recall our lives but also to help shape them: "A life story doesn't just say what happened, it says why it was important, what it means for who the person is, for who they'll become, and for what happens next." Inviting families to tell their stories provides a context for understanding a family's history as well as a glimpse into their ways of taking on the future.

Stories such as those presented here can enhance professional preparation by providing a context for theories on working with families (Prezant & Marshak, 2006; Prosser, 2009), serving as a framework for course discussions, assignments, and connections to other readings (Ludlow, Skelly, & Rohleder, 2012), and providing a catalyst for expanding students' perceptions and pre-conceived ideas about working with families (Kim & Vail, 2011). Previous studies have suggested that sharing family stories has been especially useful at reaching those who demonstrate resistance to certain values and outlooks (Kubal, Meyler, Stone, & Mauney, 2003).

The critical role of families as partners with educators has been addressed in policies such as the 2004 amendments to the Individuals with Disabilities Education Act (P.L. 108–446), and in position statements such as the Joint Position Statement on Inclusion (DEC/NAEYC, 2009). Scholars have expressed a particular appreciation and expectation for this partnering in the field of inclusive early childhood education (Blasco, 2001; Bowe, 2007; Howard, Williams, & Lepper, 2005; McWilliams, 2005; Prosser, 2009). *Conversations with Families* extends beyond early childhood, including families in various stages of parenting and children from preschool through adolescence. It offers teacher educators a resource to help foster practitioners' understanding of and capacity for partnerships with families during their professional preparation. In reading through these chapters, we hope that both teacher educators and their students will be inspired and moved to channel these families' powerful messages into their teaching practice.

References

Bayat, M. (2007). Evidence of resilience in families of children with autism. *Journal of Intellectual Disability Research*, 51(9), 702–714.

Beck, J. (2015). Life's stories. *The Atlantic*, August 10, 2015.

Blasco, P. M. (2001). *Early intervention services for infants, toddlers, and their families*. Boston: Allyn & Bacon.

Blue-Banning, M., Summers, J. A., Frankland, H. C., Nelson, L. L., & Beegle, G. (2004). Dimensions of family and professional partnerships: Constructive guidelines for collaboration. *Exceptional Children*, 70(2), 167–184.

Bowe, F. G. (2007). *Early childhood special education: Birth to eight* (4th ed.). Clifton Park, NY: Thompson Delmar Learning.

DEC/NAEYC. (2009). *Early childhood inclusion: A joint position statement of the Division for Early Childhood (DEC) and the National Association for the Education of Young Children (NAEYC)*. Chapel Hill: The University of North Carolina, FPG Child Development Institute.

Dunlap, G., & Fox, L. (2007). Parent-professional partnerships: A valuable context for addressing challenging behaviors. *International Journal of Disability, Development and Education*, 54(3), 273–285.

Gallagher, P. A., Fialka, J., Rhodes, C., & Arceneaux, C. (2002). Working with families: Rethinking denial. *Young Exceptional Children*, 5(2), 11–17.

Gallimore, R., Goldenberg, C. N., & Weisner, T. S. (1993). The social construction and subjective reality of activity settings: Implications for community psychology. *American Journal of Community Psychology*, 21, 537–559.

Gallimore, R., Weisner, T. S., Kaufman, S. Z., & Bernheimer, L. P. (1989). The social construction of ecocultural niches: Family accommodation of developmentally delayed children. *American Journal on Mental Retardation*, 94, 216–230.

Goddard, J. A., Lehr, R., & Lapadat, J. C. (2000). Parents of children with disabilities: Telling a different story. *Canadian Journal of Counseling*, 34(4), 273–289.

Goodley, D., & Tregaskis, C. (2006). Storying disability and impairment: Retrospective accounts of disabled family life. *Qualitative Health Research*, 16(5), 630–646.

Howard, V. F., Williams, B. F., & Lepper, C. (2005). *Very young children with special needs: A formative approach for today's children*. Upper Saddle River, NJ: Pearson Merrill Prentice Hall.

Kim, E. J., & Vail, C. (2011). Improving preservice teachers' perspectives on family involvement in teaching children with special needs: Guest speakers versus video. *Teacher Education and Special Education*, 34(4), 320–338.

Kubal, T., Meyler, D., Stone, R. T., & Mauney, T. T. (2003). Teaching diversity and learning outcomes: Bringing lived experience into the classroom. *Teaching Sociology*, 31, 441–455.

Lawrence-Lightfoot, S. (2016). Portraiture methodology: Blending art and science. *LEARNing Landscapes*, 9(2), 19–27.

Lawrence-Lightfoot, S., & Davis, J. H. (1997). *The art and science of portraiture*. San Francisco: Jossey-Bass.

Lee, Y.-J., Park, H., & Recchia, S. L. (2016). Embracing each other and growing together: Redefining the meaning of caregiving a child with disabilities. *Journal of Child and Family Studies*, 24(12), 3662–3675.

Ludlow, A., Skelly, C., & Rohleder, P. (2012). Challenges faced by parents of children diagnosed with autism spectrum disorder. *Journal of Health Psychology*, 17(5), 702–711.

Maul, C. A., & Singer, G. H. S. (2009). "Just good different things": Specific accommodations families make to positively adapt to their children with developmental disabilities. *Topics in Early Childhood Special Education*, 29(3), 155–170.

McWilliams, R. A. (2005). Assessing resource needs of families in context of early intervention. In M. J. Guralnick (Ed.), *The developmental systems approach to early intervention* (pp. 214–215). Baltimore, MD: Paul H. Brookes Publishing Co.

Moes, D. R., & Frea, W. D. (2000). Using family context to inform intervention planning for the treatment of a child with autism. *Journal of Positive Behavior Interventions*, 2, 40–46.

Patterson, J. M. (2002). Integrating family resilience and family stress theory. *Journal of Marriage and Family*, 64, 349–360.

Prezant, F. P., & Marshak, L. (2006). Helpful actions seen through the eyes of parents of children with disabilities. *Disability and Society*, 21(1), 31–45.

Prosser, T. M. (2009). Personnel preparation for preservice early intervention providers: Supporting families' participation in university classrooms, *Journal of Early Childhood. Teacher Education*, 30, 69–78.

Puig, V. I. (2012). Cultural and linguistic alchemy: Mining the resources of Spanish-speaking children and families receiving early intervention services. *Journal of Research in Childhood Education*, 26(3), 325–345.

Singer, G. H. S. (2006). Meta-analysis of comparative studies of depression in mothers of children with and without developmental disabilities. *American Journal of Mental Retardation*, 111, 155–169.

2

A MOTHER AND GRANDMOTHER COME TOGETHER AS CAREGIVERS

With special contributions by Rachel Williams

Entering the Williams' home is like walking into a warm family embrace. The walls and surfaces of the living room are covered with framed photos of Vivienne, her daughter Rachel, and Rachel's four children. A portrait of Vivienne and Rachel, taken when Vivienne turned 50, is particularly prominent and welcoming.

We passed through this receiving line and through the hallway, kitchen, and den to the shared heart of the home, Rassan's room. Rassan smiled broadly from his bed when he heard Rachel's voice and moaned gently when he heard mine. Just a few words of reassurance from Rachel served as enough of an endorsement for Rassan to offer me a small smile as well.

Vivienne, Rachel, and I settled into the den adjacent to Rassan's room for our interview and visit. Watching over us from the wall I faced was a cluster of photos that I interpreted to be extended family: President Barack Obama, Dr. Martin Luther King, Malcolm X, and Oprah Winfrey. A plaque of the bible quote "I can do all things through Christ who strengthens me" (Philippians 4:13) shared additional inspiration.

"We share, we share."

At the start of the interview, Vivienne identified herself as the "grandmama," described her race as "Black Jamaican" and shared her age as 61. Rachel said she was 30 years old, and identified as "African American with Jamaican descent." Vivienne included her daughter and her husband and family, and her own brothers and sisters as members of her family, Rachel's definition was a little more nuanced:

> Me, my husband, our kids. We have one kid together, and then we have Rassan, which we share, we share. I also have a daughter from, not with

him, who's nine. He has a son who's twelve, so my mother, and then his, we have his mom, his stepfather, and she has grandkids and also a five-year-old daughter as well, so, and then my aunts and uncles on the other side (laughs), so family's pretty big ... So we have Rassan, who's the oldest. Rassan's thirteen. We have Jaden, he's twelve. My daughter Leah who's nine, and Zapporah that I have with my husband, she's two.

When Rachel stated, "and then we have Rassan, which we share, we share" she looked at her mother who nodded in agreement. This chapter will primarily focus on this sharing, the ways Vivienne and Rachel come together as mother and daughter, "grandmama" and mother to share and care for Rassan.

Vivienne was born in Kingston, Jamaica, the fifth of nine children. She came to the US at the age of 17. Despite experiencing culture shock and missing her homeland, she met and married her husband and gave birth to Rachel. When Rachel was a 1 year old, Vivienne divorced and became a single mother. Vivienne has her Associate's degree in Nursing and has worked as a nurse for 37 years. Her experience in the field includes working as a Medical Surgical Nurse and an Intensive Care Unit/Critical Care Unit Charge Nurse. She is currently a Hospice Charge Nurse.

Rachel completed her Bachelor's degree and her Master of Arts degree in Early Childhood Education. She recently returned to school to earn her Master of Education degree in Inclusive Early Childhood Education. She is a kindergarten teacher during the school year and a camp director during the summers.

I first met Rachel five years ago when she was a graduate student in my course "Families, Communities and Schools: Diversity, Culture and Democracy." As a course assignment, students were required to interview a family to learn about their unique culture, strengths, resources, goals, and priorities. In their assigned papers they were to share this family's story and outline a brief support plan responsive to the family's identified goals and priorities. Rachel spoke to me after class to ask if she could use her own family as the focus of her paper. She explained that when she was in high school she had a son, Rassan, who was born with schizencephaly, a rare developmental disorder characterized by abnormal slits or clefts in the cerebral hemispheres of the brain. Individuals with clefts in both hemispheres commonly have developmental delays, delays in speech and language skills, seizures, and problems with brain-spinal cord communication. Since his birth, Rassan has lived with her mother as his primary caregiver, but now that Rachel is older, married, and has other children, she wanted to use this assignment as an opportunity to talk to her mother about ways they may re-negotiate their roles in caring for Rassan. This chapter will draw on how Rachel captured and reflected on that conversation in her paper and these excerpts are cited as "Assignment, 2014." In a subsequent course Rachel took with me when she returned to the university to earn a Master of Education degree in Inclusive Education, Rachel expanded on this work by continuing to examine her family's evolving roles and goals, resources, and priorities. This time she also included her husband and daughter in the conversation as she looked back to reflect on her family's experiences and looked forward to imagine their future. Excerpts and insights shared from this paper are cited as "Assignment, 2019." All other information shared will be from the in-person interview I conducted with Vivienne and Rachel, with their shared Rassan, in the next room.

"But I can always remember you being there."

Rachel began her paper entitled, "The Life and Times of the Williams Family" in this way: "Sometimes your life can change so drastically that it may leave you to believe all is lost and that everything from that moment will be heartache. I am here to tell a story about a mother and daughter and how their lives changed many years ago …" (Assignment, 2014). As we hear this story unfold, in Rachel and Vivienne's words, we'll see that, indeed, their lives have changed, but everything that followed was not heartache.

Vivienne described to Rachel her experience as a single mother in this way: "I was a single mother raising an only child. It was not easy, I had the help of my family but my daughter was my responsibility. I sacrificed so much. There was so much I wanted but I always put you first. I wanted you to be exposed to a variety of things. I wanted you to be the best" (Assignment, 2014).

Vivienne looked back at what she called "the most trying year of my life." She had lost her father, undergone major surgery, and, as the year drew to a close, she learned of Rachel's pregnancy. During our conversation she remembered her feelings at hearing the news:

> It was hard because when I found that Rachel was pregnant, it was already six months, so it's like your whole world turned upside down at that point, it was kind of shocking. It was hurtful, you're angry, but you didn't have time to be angry because the next step was a week after … (we learned) the baby had a brain injury in utero. So now all of that put aside and let's focus on her. And now what next? … We're kind of running around for genetic counseling, went to CHOP (Children's Hospital of Philadelphia) trying to find out what went wrong with the baby.

Vivienne reflected on the messages they were receiving from the medical professionals around them:

> All the news from the doctors were so bad. We went from doctor to doctor. The advice given to us was to go to another country and abort the baby at 6 months. I remember sitting there frozen and thinking we are not going to do this, where there is life there is hope and I knew from then on I had to be there for you and we had to take it one day at a time. (Assignment, 2014)

And those days before Rassan's birth were difficult as Vivienne grew increasingly concerned for her unborn grandchild's health and also Rachel's emotional state:

> I would just sit here night after night and hear her crying in her room, just crying ... and I'm praying, give me another word for encouraging her, you know, and going to work at the same time, doing everything at the same time.

Vivienne remembered an experience she had during that time:

> I remember going into the baby store to look for some clothes for her and for the baby, and I freaked out. I had to run out the store. I couldn't breathe, I couldn't catch my breath. It's like I had this anxiety ... I just dropped everything and left the store.

Rachel's memories of this time are limited, but her recollections of her mother's presence are very telling:

> My mind is so blank. I think I try to dismiss all the bad – but I can always remember you being there. (Assignment, 2014)

Looking back at this time, one medical professional, in particular, stands out. Dr. G. was Rachel's gynecologist; her words and the pain that they inflicted are still easily accessible 14 years later. During several of the pre-natal visits, Vivienne remembers her saying:
"You know, he's not going to live ... You know he's going to be a vegetable."
She recalls:

> It was very hurting but, you know, this time I was more focusing on her and trying to just dismiss this doctor ... you know, I just didn't like to make waves, especially so close to the birth ... the last thing she said to me ... she said she's not going to monitor the baby coming out of the womb ... because it's gonna be stillborn anyway.

As a nurse, and a mother, and a soon-to-be grandmama, Vivienne knew this was wrong, but she directed her energy into caring for and shielding Rachel, and she called on her religious faith and "just started praying." Two nights before Rassan was born, Rachel went into the hospital with labor pains. Dr. G told her that it would be another three weeks before she went into labor and sent her home. When Rachel returned two days later, on Christmas Day, she learned that Dr. G. had gone on vacation and another doctor would be delivering the baby. Vivienne was certain "this is all God's move."

She recalls the attending doctor reading from Rachel's chart, "He probably didn't know I was standing behind him, and he said, 'Oh, she expects me not to monitor this baby.' And he just said it out loud."

But he did not heed Dr. G's counsel:

> He had the NICU nurses, the ventilator – everybody was ready to go once the baby come out, which was fine with me and I appreciate that because that's showing that he's concerned and he's going to take every step to help this child. So when the baby came out … I was standing over her bed and I said, Lord, the only thing I'm asking you, I'm not going to be naïve, I know the situation, but if I could just hear a cry, that's all I ask. Just let me hear a cry when this baby come out. And that baby came out crying, crying, crying, crying, crying. And they did not put him on a respirator. He stayed about a half a day or a day in the NICU no oxygen, and in three days he went home with her.

Listening to her mother talk about Rassan's birth, Rachel responded to her:

> I think this was the scariest day of my life and far more the most difficult. I never knew that you had all these thoughts and that you were so scared. It's almost as if you were having a baby too in some sense. (Assignment, 2014)

Rachel remembers Rassan's arrival with tenderness and conviction:

> He was the cutest baby I had ever seen. I heard him cry and then I saw the doctors carry him away. He was healthy and alive. Although I knew he would be developmentally challenged and life would not be easy, I was happy that he was alive and present despite all I had been told. At that moment I knew my life had changed forever. I knew things would never be the same. The one thing I did know was that I needed to do everything I could to make sure he would be great. (Assignment, 2019)

Vivienne recalls an early memory and her clear satisfaction when she shares the first and only visit Rassan had with Dr. G:

> I swear Rassan see this lady … she came out and she's looking down at him, and Rassan looking up at her with his little glasses, and I swear the baby went like this: 'Hmm!!' She pulled back, she actually pulled back!

Both Vivienne and Rachel still lament at the "lack of compassion and empathy" they experienced from medical professionals during Rachel's pregnancy. Rachel commented that, at the time, due to her age and state of overwhelm, she dismissed what the doctors were saying. But now being older, and more mature, and a professional herself, she sees how inappropriate and hurtful it was. She added that she thinks many of the professionals' responses were influenced by their biases regarding "age, race and statistics."

After Rassan's birth, the Social Worker at the hospital recognized Rachel's depressive state and the strong bond between Vivienne and Rachel. She listened carefully and included in her recommendations the suggestion that Vivienne do her best to send Rachel back to dance school. Vivienne credits Rachel's return to dance class with pulling her out of her depression. Rachel's return to her public performing arts high school was less healing; her classmates were judgmental and unkind. She explains that, at the time, she was timid and just "stuffed it up" but that now she knows how to defend herself and Rassan.

Rachel remembers that it was also difficult for her to navigate changes at home:

> I remember when he was born … I was very jealous … My mother … calls him Ray-Ray, so at the time, I used to be Ray-Ray, then it was taken from me, and then, you know, all the attention went on him … I went from Ray-Ray to Rachel … now he's getting all the attention and where do I stand, you know?

Vivienne chimed in:

> I remember one time I was singing …"You are my sunshine, my only sunshine" to Rassan, and one day she got so upset. "That's not Rassan's song! That's my song! You have to find a song for Rassan."

From that day on "Twinkle, Twinkle, Little Star" became Rassan's song and Rachel regained her status as Vivienne's "only sunshine"! As a mother now, Rachel recognizes the ways her own children can be jealous when her attention is directed to another sibling.

"A heart so pure and sweet."

Rachel shares Rassan's medical history:

> Months after Rassan's birth, his head started growing rapidly due to hydrocephalus, a buildup of fluid in the ventricles deep within the brain. Rassan has had five hip surgeries. He has a ventricular, peritoneal shunt that was placed in the back of his head at five months old. He has been hospitalized for pneumonia on numerous occasions. Rassan has poor vision. He had a feeding tube placed in two years ago because he was unable to handle a pureed diet. He currently attends a school for disabled children and is accompanied by a nurse 7am to 7pm daily. (Assignment, 2019)

She also describes his temperament and ways of communicating:

> Despite his ups and downs, Rassan has a heart so pure and sweet. He loves to laugh. He loves to hear familiar voices. Although he is unable to walk or talk he has feelings like anyone else. He will cry to tell you when he is upset. (Assignment, 2019)

Rachel, Vivienne, and Rachel's 9-year-old daughter, Leah, all commented on how it makes them feel when people stare at Rassan in public:

VIVIENNE: It hurts. It does not always feel good. I tell them he is just like you and that he has feelings too. I think people should just educate themselves. He is not the only disabled person in the world. (Assignment, 2014)

RACHEL: I used to feel bad for Rassan when people stared. Now I just embrace it. When people stare I take Rassan's hand and allow him to wave. I do experience a lot of people telling me God bless you and that I know it is not easy and I am praying for you. That makes me feel good. (Assignment, 2014)

LEAH: Sometimes people look at him weird when we go out, but it doesn't bother me anymore. Mommy told me to tell people to say hi to him, and to remind them that he is just like anyone else, and he does not like when you stare at him. (Assignment, 2019)

Rachel talked more about what she'd like people to understand about Rassan:

> He's human like everybody else. He has his own personality … When he hears new voices, he gets upset – he doesn't like it … He can't control the things that are happening to him but … he knows his surroundings. He doesn't like to go outside, he gets very agitated … He knows his comfort zone, he knows the people around him, and he can recognize voices. Just to know he's just like everybody else. You can't make people feel comfortable, some people, that's just how they are. They feel like if they have to hold him, they'll break him or something, 'cause they're not used to him … Just treat him right, and that, you know, we should all help each other out. Just to know that he's regular, he has his own personality, and he's not, he's not dumb.

The apparent discomfort and fear that Rachel described is not limited to people they meet in public. Vivian explains that even her family demonstrates it:

> And even my family having a hard time even dealing with Rassan. I can't get my family to watch him. My sisters … can't watch him. They're afraid … so it's like I never get that support. I can get the talking part … Many times I want to go someplace, I call my sister, 'Can you?' 'Oh, I have things to do.' But I know they don't have things to do … they're just kind of scared …

When they see him, they talk to him as long as I'm around, but that's as far as it goes. But I'd just like people to know that he's just a kid like any other kid, but he just can't do the things that normal kids do, you know?

Rachel also discussed her extended family's limited understanding of Rassan:

I'm not always in the mood to educate, especially if we're having one of our more challenging days. Sometime I feel like a broken record, wishing I could just hand out a brochure to all the aunts and uncles and distant cousins who have questions over holiday dinners ... Many times I always get the same questions, "So what is life going to be like for Rassan now? Can he go to 'regular' school? Will he ever learn to talk?" (Assignment, 2019)

"Peace and comfort in hard times."

Rachel and Vivienne recognize that their family is rich in resources. Vivienne's experience as a nurse and Rachel's academic background and experience in education help them understand Rassan's needs and advocate for him with other professionals. They have established strong partnerships with Rassan's educational and medical providers.

Rachel explained that Rassan is currently in a school for children with disabilities. She praised the staff's patience and their ongoing systems for keeping communication between home and school flowing. She appreciates the events they have for families and the specialized equipment they provide for the children including augmentative and alternative communication devices.

Another resource Rachel and Vivienne value is that Rassan currently has a nurse for 12 hours a day. Because the same nurses spend time with Rassan at home and in school this also enhances the partnership between them and the professionals that help care for Rassan. Rachel and Vivienne have also learned how to work with social workers, insurance providers, and various social service organizations to access critical supplies for Rassan. They are also always very grateful for Rassan's periods of good health.

When asked about their family's greatest resources, Rachel responded with quick conviction, "well, number one, my mother's a strength." Throughout her assignments and our discussion, she referred to her mother as her "hero," "saving grace," "backbone and strength," "everyone's superman" and "... a fighter ... (who) only sees the beauty in Rassan. She is a great support who coaches and cheers. She is my Warrior Grandmother who gives unconditional, unending love." (Assignment 2019)

Vivienne identifies her "church family" and God's grace as ongoing sources of her strength. She explains that the fact that Rachel's husband, Jonathan, is so supportive puts her mind at ease. Jonathan's flexible work schedule allows him to help bring Rassan to doctor appointments. He visits with Rassan, cuts his hair every other Saturday, and has learned how to care for Rassan. Jonathan reflects on his commitment to Rachel, Rassan, and the rest of their family:

> I knew life would not be ordinary, but I also knew that I was blessed to have Rassan in my life because he helped teach me patience and unconditional love. I must admit that at times being husband, and a step father of a special needs child, can be challenging to stay focused when the challenges of caregiving collide with the needs of my wife and other children. (Assignment, 2019)

Jonathan muses about what it would be like to play sports with Rassan and his other son, Jaydon, who are nearly the same age, but says that he has found other ways to connect with Rassan. He expresses his resolve in this way:

> It's been my observation that many men are overwhelmed by the responsibility of being husbands and fathers and from the very first day I met Rassan, I knew that there was no time to be overwhelmed, and that I had to be the strength and support for this family when they would need it most. (Assignment, 2019)

Rachel summarizes her family's strengths poignantly:

> Our major strength and resource are how we counsel frequently with the Lord through prayer and scripture study. Our spiritual connection allows us to find peace and comfort in hard times. I have also learned all I can about Rassan's disability. We have … (learned) from numerous professionals and reliable sources of information about Rassan's disability. Over the years I have talked with other parents who share my values and who have similar struggles. This has helped me understand my own feelings and provided me valuable support. To strengthen our family, we have explained Rassan's disability to our children and other family members. We have learned to be patient with one another as we adjust to new challenges and changes. We have not allowed Rassan's disability to become the focus of all family activities. We do things that are special to Rassan, but we also do other activities that meet the needs of our other children. Whenever possible, we do things that include all family members. I am learning to strengthen myself and find time to relax away from the constant demands that are required. I am strengthening my marriage by spending time with my husband and doing things that we both enjoy. I learned that my biggest strength is striving to keep Rassan from harm. I learned to play into Rassan's strengths and treat him as normally as possible. I strive to provide Rassan with every opportunity to develop his skills, talents, and abilities. (Assignment, 2019)

"You taught me well, I can do it."

When Rachel interviewed her mother for the assignment in 2014, she broached the subject of transitioning their roles in caring for Rassan:

RACHEL: You have been taking care of Rassan for 9 years. I have graduated high school, and college and am currently working on my masters. I am married and also have a daughter who is 5 years old. How do you feel about me taking Rassan full time and possibly moving out of state?

VIVIENNE: The only thing I can tell you is that Rassan is a lot of work. You need the resources and when you move you will have no one who knows him or his history. In the long run, Rassan will suffer. When a situation around him changes he will know the difference. It is a 24-hour job and I think you need to think about making drastic steps. You have to ask yourself is this really what you want right now in your life … I can only take things one day at a time. I cannot see for tomorrow. I have to live for today.

RACHEL: I think you are scared of change. It frightens you to know that one day Rassan will leave you or that I am not ready to take care of him on my own. I notice that every time I talk about moving away and taking him full-time you dismiss it. Things will have to change, Mommy, and I believe you deserve a break and to live your life. You taught me well, I can do it.

During our interview together, Rachel and Vivienne reflected on the conversation they had five years earlier. Vivienne had recently re-read Rachel's assignment and commented:

> … when she said that there's gonna come a day when she has to … take Rassan … I worried about that part. Because I don't know how she would. maybe she would do it if I'm not here … she would have no choice … And I'm thinking about her with the other three kids and then thinking, where would Rassan fit into … I would see where she would have to probably end up staying home. And even talking about moving, and I'm thinking of all the set-up that he has here, it would all have to start all over again, and it's not easy …

While Rachel and Vivienne have not yet created a plan for transitioning their roles of caring for Rassan, it's clear that they are joined in their love and commitment for each other and Rassan. Rachel summarized it in this way:

> Rassan will always be cared for and loved. My mother wants me to be fully prepared and have things in order for when the day comes and I have full responsibility of Rassan. She promised to always be there for all of us for as long as she can. I am now researching and finding as many resources as I can for Rassan especially since adulthood is quickly approaching for him. I know

many things will change for him once he turns 18, and I want to be fully equipped to handle all the changes. I have my husband's full support, my kids are very loving and helpful, and my mom has helped instill in me all the important things I need to know. Our life is not a fairytale, each day is a new adventure, but being surrounded by a vast amount of support and love gets me through each day. (Assignment, 2019)

This sentiment is echoed by Leah, Rachel's 9-year-old:

I really love my brother, and I love helping grandma with him. Grandma taught me how to do lots of things for him, so one day when she cannot do it anymore we will all know how to help him. (Assignment, 2019)

"Open his hand and hold mine."

Rachel and Vivienne acknowledged that they have had to let go of some of the goals they had for Rassan and that there are times when they succumb to feeling discouraged and anxious about the future. But Vivienne invites gratitude to take up the space where previous goals resided:

When he was younger, I was hoping that he would be able to do more, like … say words. But now, I just thank God for each day. I just want him to stay well. Whatever progression he makes, I'm grateful … if he can just open his hand and hold mine, I'm grateful … I'm just grateful for who he is right now and that he's here, you know.

Rachel holds onto the goal that she will sometime soon take on the role of raising Rassan full time. Integrated into this is her dream of opening her own center. She imagines working alongside Rassan and her mother in a "Child Center Dome" where diverse children can learn and develop in active ways and creating a curriculum that is responsive to children's and families' expectations and goals.

One day at a time and step by step are the refrains that Rachel and Vivienne offer as advice to other families. They urge them to also remember that there are always others experiencing greater difficulties. Given the chance to speak to professionals, Vivienne would offer the following counsel:

I would have to let them know that every child is different and you have to meet that child wherever that child is … and you have to treat them as human and just show them the same love and concern and compassion, you know. You can't just mark that child off because they're different … And I think a lot of people do that … They write these kids off too quick and they don't show them that love and patience … I'd like them to learn … patience and understanding.

Rachel distilled the advice: "I would tell them if they don't have the patience or heart, they should find a different career."

As Rachel and Vivienne considered how they would advise professionals, memories of Dr. G, Rachel's gynecologist during her pregnancy with Rassan, and her attitude and actions once again swelled to the surface. Vivienne seized on the invitation to imagine what she would say if she could speak to her today:

> I'm so mad with her, I'd probably tell her just the plain truth. I'd say ... when my daughter was coming to you, I think you were very mean and unkind in the things you were saying to a sixteen-year-old ... I'd say, you didn't show much of a concern for her feelings, even for this baby that she was carrying. You wanted to get rid of that child so fast 'cause when you told the doctor not to monitor this baby, you're telling me that you didn't care ... You don't know what was going on with that baby that probably could have taken her life, and if you're not monitoring to see what's happening with that baby inside her, that could have taken her life as well. So you didn't have ... that type of caring attitude that a doctor should have for his patient, regardless of what you know about this baby ... Your call is to do everything you can for that patient and for that baby, and when you're done, you can say ... I did everything I can ... just like I tell nurses ... When you leave ... you should be able to look back and say, I did everything I could for that patient. I put my whole in my work today. I probably would have to tell her a lot more than that ... No empathy, no concern, unkind, mean ... And even you know I could have sued you too, but thank God I was a different person.

Rachel and Vivienne shared that they have learned a great deal from Rassan. They both highlighted patience and Vivienne discussed that she's learned to be grateful for little things. She explained that she thinks Rassan's smile speaks as a lesson, "Like listen, just wipe that frown off your face, just wipe that depression off ... like that's what he's trying to tell you with that smile. Just get rid of all of that." Rachel stated that, through Rassan, she has learned the strength of a mother's love. I believe she was referencing herself as both the source and recipient of that love.

I was able to coax Vivienne and Rachel to consider ways they felt proud of themselves. Rachel discussed the sacrifices and commitment that she has made to pursue her education, invest in her career, provide for her family, and cook dinner every night! Vivienne explained that if she were to leave this world now she would feel that she had accomplished something by helping her daughter get so far. She is also proud that she has been a nurse for over 30 years and she described her life as comprised of her job, grandkids, Rassan, and church.

"Big dreams."

Our interview ended with the following exchange:

INTERVIEWER: Is there anything else you want to say to each other?

RACHEL: Thank you for always being there, you know, doing what you do. Say if you really get tired and you can't do it no more ... let us know ... And I know Rassan's grateful and he's comfortable.

VIVIENNE: (pause) And I thank you for being my daughter.

RACHEL: Awww.

INTERVIEWER: She's your sunshine, your only sunshine.

VIVIENNE: ... So yeah, she is my sunshine, she's my only child, and I do everything I have to do for her, you know, to see her through the rough times, the hard times, you know, and I love her. It's just who we are, we support each other.

INTERVIEWER: It sounds like you deserve each other – and that's a good thing!

VIVIENNE: It's a good thing, it's a good thing. She gave me a lot of headache when she's growing up, but it's a good thing ... But she was very ambitious.

INTERVIEWER: She's still got lots of big dreams.

RACHEL: Big dreams.

Questions for Discussion

1. How would you describe the Williams family's strengths and resources?
2. How would you characterize the Williams family's communication and collaboration with professionals?
3. How do Rachel and her mother negotiate their roles as Rassan's caregivers?
4. Rachel states that she thinks many of the professionals' responses were influenced by their biases regarding "age, race and statistics." Consider examples of this from the story. As a professional, what can you do to challenge your own misconceptions and avoid enacting negative stereotypes?

3

A MOTHER LEARNS TO ADVOCATE FOR A PRESCHOOLER WITH COMPLEX NEEDS

I first met Alicia and Juan Pablo in my role as faculty director of a university-affiliated child care center when Juan Pablo, 2 years old, was entering our toddler room. Over the course of the next year, our relationship continued as Juan Pablo began to receive early intervention services both at home and in the classroom. At his 3-year-old Committee on Preschool Special Education (CPSE) evaluation, a self-contained setting was recommended and he transitioned to a special education classroom at another school. Alicia was quick to respond when asked if she would like to participate in the Family Conversations project over a year after Juan Pablo left our center. I scheduled her interview soon after.

We met in my office at the college, sitting across from each other at a small table. Alicia gave signed permission to record our conversation, which was loosely guided by the interview protocol designed for the project. The conversation flowed freely for the most part, providing Alicia the opportunity to share her thoughts and feelings about parenting and family life with Juan Pablo, the story of her journey thus far, and some of her hopes and goals for the future.

In response to the opening question, Alicia described her family:

> We're a small family. Actually myself, my husband, and then my four-year-old, Juan Pablo … We're older, in my early fifties. My husband is in his late forties. And after trying really, really hard —and also with the help of science— we were able to then have our four-year-old, our child … We've just been married ten years, and so we said, well, at least let's try for one and we did. And that's our family. So really small, living here in New York City in a real New York type environment, meaning small apartment, five-floor walk-up …

Asked about other important people in their family's life, Alicia said: "Unfortunately, our family is really small and very limited, really." She shared that both of her parents had died recently, and that even though she has multiple siblings, it was her mother that she was closest to.

> … my mother in particular was a source of a lot of support where I was calling her, literally every day three times a day just for anything and everything. So once she died … I realized it became clear, I mean my mother was my, is my best friend … my whole world was built around my mother, even though I have an extended family with, including myself, six brothers and sisters … We're all mainly concentrated in Florida or California. I'm the only one in New York City. But with her death, instead of us coming closer … really the family structure has disappeared.

"I have to be really, really careful with who I really talk to about these things."

In further discussing non-familial supports, Alicia talked about her culture as Cuban-American as perhaps part of the reason that she does not have close friends that she feels comfortable talking to in depth about Juan Pablo:

> … I'm Cuban American, born in Cuba but raised in the U.S. and I, maybe because of my cultural upbringing or the way I was brought up, we're really a very (pause) I have friends, but not friends, for example, that I can reach out to and really sit down and talk to about these issues.

She talked about her husband's family, whom she feels closer to than her own siblings in some ways, but they all live in a small town in Spain. They also have a different attitude about the need for early intervention, preferring to wait and see what happens over time.

> They're all in Spain, so that, you know, the distance doesn't help and also then it's, it's culturally, I think, how we deal with these issues, these challenges that we, any family can have with their children is very different. For them, it is an idea that, well, instead of speaking now, wait until they're ten years old …

Alicia shared that even one of her international colleagues at the college told her that in Spain, there is much less awareness about autism. She said:

> Well, in Spain, it's just now people are becoming aware of what that is because that doesn't even exist. It does exist but it's not something that you read about, hear about much, or that people know what to do with it.

Alicia summed it up by saying: "So the support that we have in our family when it comes to Juan Pablo is not really a lot. So … I reach out to my colleagues … or other parents who have similar challenges." She added:

> … And in a way, even though, you know, my son does have a diagnosis of autism spectrum … I fluctuate in terms of do I really share this information with just anybody? I really don't, I find, and I really, just speaking freely without feeling that I will be judged by it or not, I believe in trying to overcome autism. So I belong to that school, so that I have to be really, really careful with who I really talk to about these things. In Juan Pablo's case, you know, his autism is—you see one kid with autism and that's all you see, one kid with autism. You can't really generalize, you know …

"I'm knocking on wood because he has come a very long way."

As Alicia continued to talk about Juan Pablo's diagnosis of autism, she further explained her ambivalent feelings about the label, and how it can be difficult to understand what it actually means for her own child. She is inspired by all the progress he has made since he started receiving services, and hopeful about his future. She shared:

> I'm very thankful and I'm knocking on wood because he has come a very long way. He still has the diagnosis, it hasn't, it won't go away, but when I began this whole journey…
>
> I remember one of the first reports I received with, with the words "severe autism," and at that time, you know, I just, I cried … one of our colleagues had recommended that I have a glass of wine near me, and thank God I did because I really (laughs) … needed it at that moment. And … just a lot of reflection, thinking, sitting by myself and trying to process this, you know? Because he did fit the bill. He wasn't speaking, he was babbling a lot, he wasn't paying attention … you couldn't really get his attention in any way. When you would put him with other kids, he was, you know, doing his own thing. But now, after two years of … working really hard with all kinds of occupational therapists, speech and language therapists, all kinds of support systems, he's now speaking, he's actually speaking, making his needs known.

She added:

> … But is he so-called cured? No … you know, autism will be a label he will always carry with him. But if he can then learn how to … yes, he will learn how to live with it in the mainstream society, that is what I mean by over-coming it. Not that he will get rid of that label, but at least … I can still have

a dream of him going to college, graduating, maybe perhaps get married if he ever wants to get married, having his own family.

Reflecting further on possibilities for the future, Alicia shared her hope that Juan Pablo will be able to live independently. Although he is still very young, being an older parent makes her more aware of how soon this time may come. She shared:

> ... with older parents is our concern that our time is limited ... I realize that my finality will be sooner rather than later ... I have friends who have kids now that are entering college, about my age, you know, and I realize that if I live, and I hope that I live for that, that will be really a blessing ... and so I really want to prepare him, I mean that's always in the back of my mind, prepare him to be independent and be able to really handle the world on his own.

"Do we pigeonhole him into being special ed? Is this a label he will have for the rest of his life?"

As she came to the realization that Juan Pablo would need extra help to reach these goals, Alicia felt the responsibility was on her to make educational decisions for him. Although her husband was involved in his care, he had a different sense about Juan Pablo's development.

> ... one thing I haven't mentioned is that when Juan Pablo received the diagnosis, it was really, you know, it was really just me dealing with this because although I have a husband, he does not believe that our child has some challenges—I mean, he realizes that there's something different about our child and I really practice avoidance of the conversation at home if we want to maintain peace ... So as long as our child can sort of act as so-called normal as my husband thinks he needs to be, that is an issue that I don't have to deal with.

She went on to talk more about how she ultimately made the decision to go forward with choosing a self-contained special education classroom for Juan Pablo, despite her initial fears about "pigeonholing" him.

> ... my biggest concern at that time was, you know, do I, do we pigeonhole him into being special ed and is this a label that he will have for the rest of his life, with all kinds of concerns, maybe real and unreal, about what special ed means? ... or do I bite the bullet ... and give him, my child, the opportunity to experience, you know, a special ed environment, and give it a try, you know? See ... the progress he would make or not in that environment. And without really letting a lot of time pass because, you know, when you have these challenges, you need to nip this in the bud the earlier the better, instead of sitting around waiting for it to get better on its own.

Alicia talked about how difficult it was for her to visit special education pre-school programs, imagining Juan Pablo in one of the classrooms:

> … and it was heartbreaking because you would go there, you'd see kids with all kinds of challenges, and you, you know, you try to think of your kid, remember, I'm thinking of my kid as one day he'll be normal, and whether he'll really do this on his own, but you see those kids and, and keeping in mind that autism is just different for everybody, so you see kids that are, you know, I don't, I don't know how to say this, but worse off than my son is.

"But in the back of my mind, there's always that question: Does he really have autism?"

After seeing Juan Pablo's progress, Alicia was feeling better about the educational decisions she had made for him so far. She talked about some of the things that have gone especially well for him over the past year in the following way: "He's making his wishes known … I can call his name, he's now going to pay attention to me. He will see somebody and he knows what to say. Hi, my name is Juan Pablo." Although she sees that her son still has some learning challenges that have not been resolved, Alicia remains ambivalent about his diagnosis of autism. She says, "… in my mind, yes, he does have autism and I'm living with a child with autism, and I can say it to you right now …" Yet, there is still that lingering question: "But in the back of my mind, there's always that question: Does he really have autism?"

As she reflected on Juan Pablo's learning over time, she began to analyze his progress in this light: "… the babble was always there, because there are other kids that are not even doing that. But he was babbling … and then he went into a stage of echolalia." It wasn't until he was about 3 years old that "he really started putting words together in many sentences and phrases and making his needs known." But again, she raises the question about whether Juan Pablo may simply be on his own neuro-developmental path:

> And how did that happen, I don't know. I would like to say it was the school, and … in the back of my mind, there's still that question of what's really going on … is there something neurologically that is, you know, his neurons are getting more mature and he's just at that age where for him, it's clicking, and it's coming together …

As our conversation continued, Alicia shared more about how she is always wondering what really contributes to Juan Pablo's learning. She talked about the trip she took with him last summer, and the positive impact it seemed to have. After a very stressful year of both negotiating Juan Pablo's services and enduring her mother's death, Alicia decided she needed a break and took Juan Pablo to visit his father's family in Spain.

... my son was scheduled to enter summer school with special ed, and up to
then I had seen lots of progress ... But I said I need a break and I just ...
broke protocol and expectations, and I said I am leaving (pause) and I'm
taking him with me for the summer. And I went off to Spain.

Although she knew that a break was what she needed for herself, she was
worried that this decision on her part might not be the best for Juan Pablo.

And I thought with that decision ... he will have some regression here
because for the summer now ... I was going to put him in a new challenging
language situation because the Spanish family doesn't speak any English, and
here I was, I took him out, and literally we were there a month and a half.
We just went to Spain.

She talked about the disruptions to his routine that the trip brought about
and how he had no choice but to adapt to the changes in food choices and
daily activities: "And he had to, you know, I was tired, so I was like just deal
with it! He's a finicky eater, part of the diagnosis is sensory issues ... I just
didn't care. We were there." She was pleasantly surprised to see the progress
Juan Pablo continued to make in spite of these dramatic changes to his routine. "And, you know, after we came back from Spain is when he started
talking."

Seeing this positive change in Juan Pablo's communication skills after being
out of school and in a new environment for the whole summer seemed to add
to Alicia's confusion about both his diagnosis and his learning style. She said,
"So I was like I don't know what happened, so that's why I have misgivings.
Misgivings is probably ... it's too strong of a word, but I wonder what it is he
has?" She went on to share her thoughts about the timing of introducing Juan
Pablo to things:

... when is the right time to put him in, because I'm finding just from
observing him that there's a right time. Maybe I've been sort of pushing,
pushing, pushing which is good, but for him there's a time when he's going
to start speaking, he'll start speaking. When he's going to start paying attention to something, he's going to start paying attention to it. And maybe it's
connected developmentally ...

She talked about the fact that her son is very big and tall for his age, "so there's a
lot of expectations for him" but he's still very young. She went on to say that
even now at 4 years old "he goes outside and he wants to hold Mommy's
hand ... I see other kids that are just running around wild, but he wants to stay
next to Mommy."

"But it's, I just have to say with time. With time."

It seemed from all that Alicia was sharing that she was revising her thinking about how to respond to Juan Pablo's needs. She talked about a change she had made to better facilitate his sleeping, which has been an ongoing problem since he was very young.

> ... yes, we live in a small apartment but I did buy a full over full bunk bed ... for the bedroom, but he still wants to sleep with Mommy in her bed. And yes, I mean, you can sort of deal with these issues (pause) ... this is the way it is and go to your top bed. But it's, I just have to say with time. With time. That's one of the things I've learned with this process, just support, be as supportive as you can, and ... just back off a little. Back off.

In dialogue with me, Alicia shared more about her own new insights.

INTERVIEWER: And when you went to Spain you kind of got out of your routine, too, right? So, in a sense, you freed up something.
ALICIA: Yes! Yes. I did. Yes.
INTERVIEWER: For yourself as well as for him.
ALICIA: Yes, I think of that too because I tried to play it cool and tried to play it, you know, as professional as possible, and warm, though, at the same time ... but I realized that maybe I'm giving off some neurons ... that he picks up!

"So I thought about what can I change with myself."

Adding further to her thoughts about Juan Pablo's growing communicative competence, Alicia shared some changes that she had made within the family's daily lives.

> I feel the other thing that's going well is I feel a little bit more empowered as a parent in terms of, you know, even before our son came, we're not a very talkative family. And there's lots of literature and research on that, especially when you look at the socioeconomic background of parents, certain socio-economic parents speak more to their kids and others don't. And so, I am very cognizant of that and I try to be different. But even before our kid came, we weren't a very talkative family. (laughs) ... my husband is who he is and the way he is, and I am the way I am, and you know, I can't change him. So I thought about what can I change with myself.

She went on to say that growing up in her own family, these kinds of conversations were not modeled. Her mother was talkative, but her father was quiet and because of his long and irregular work hours at the factory, family dinners were not a daily event.

My mother was always an excellent cook and there was always food in the house, and she was none of this going to McDonald's or anything like that. She was cooking food and there was always food … but … we would come home and grab your plate and literally it wasn't about now sit down and talk to me about your day. Everybody would go to their rooms and would eat their food in their rooms and start their homework.

Alicia spoke about her early life in Cuba, where her father had been in prison for ten years "because he spoke out against the government." The oldest children in her family, including herself, were born during this time – "because of the conjugal rights, that's how we were born." Her mother was able to manage because they owned a small apartment and "she had an extended, really big family, thirteen brothers and sisters … so they were helping her too … because … there was no money at that time." After her father was released, her family left Cuba as political refugees in the late 1960s and came to the mid-western United States:

> … I was seven years old at that time, and so I was a child, and that's where we headed, to Indiana. And why Indiana? Because there was a church in Indiana, an Episcopal church that sponsored us out of Cuba, and so we ended up in Indiana and, you know, my mother, it was a hard place to be because it was an industrial town, and at that time, right now there's only one steel mill working. At that time when we arrived, there were still five. And so it was just a grey, depressing place.

As the conversation continued, Alicia shared: "… my father didn't speak a word of English and neither did we" but after some time he was able to find work in the steel mills. She expressed her family's gratitude for the church's help: "… it was a blessing and it was because, you know … the church really took care of us, we had an apartment. Then we moved into a house." She said that her father always told them, "My job is to go to the steel mills. Your job is to study …," deeply instilling the value of education in his children. "He would say, Education … will give you whatever you need …" and saved money so that as they got older the children could attend private schools.

Finding her way back to her thoughts about socio-economic differences in the ways that parents communicate with their children, Alicia remembered how she observed these differences at the private school she attended, where she was one of 5 students of color out of 300.

> And I could see the way the parents would interact with their kids … then I read in graduate school about, you know, the differences, I could, I could see it … Because our family, not that … we weren't speaking, but it was just, it was different. My father, my mother, were very traditional in terms of roles,

and so when they did speak, it was about the memories of Cuba that still remain with me. You know, Cuba, when my father was home, it was all about Cuba, all about the family they had left there, and trying to send extra money to them. And so the language also played a role, if you kept your Spanish, you were able to be part of this conversation. But if you didn't, like my younger brothers and sisters, three that were born here in the U.S., you know, they were sort of left out of that whole conversation.

"Everybody needs to clap for themselves."

Throughout our conversation, Alicia often referred to herself as the parent who is responsible for negotiating Juan Pablo's educational needs. She is the one who sought early intervention services for him when her husband did not feel they were needed, and she is the one who has continued to follow through with intervention program recommendations to meet Juan Pablo's needs. As we talked about the strengths of their family, Alicia reflected on the words of a special education advocate that she keeps going back to:

> ... she said ... this is not an easy journey that you're on ... and it's thankless because no one is going to thank you for what you're doing for your child ... everybody needs to clap for themselves because nobody's going to do that, nobody will see the hours, the hours that you pour into this ...

Although she said she was not exactly clapping for herself, she added: "if it wasn't because of the concern and the seriousness I take this and the love for my child, it would be a whole totally different game." In response to the question about family strengths she said,

> I don't want to say myself, but it is (pause) it is. My husband, again, doesn't believe my son has a problem, so he was going to wait it out until he was ten years old. I don't have close family members here that even, that even know he has this ... I have to watch my words with everybody ... The ones in Spain ... think that he has an issue, a behavior issue, that we're too permissive with him.

Thinking back on her own experiences as Juan Pablo's parent, Alicia talked about the importance of believing in your child and drawing on what can be learned from research as well as the strengths of others who have been on a similar path:

> ... other people have walked, not the same but a similar sort of route, and there's lots of written material out there about what is working, not working, the latest research ... you have to grab all of this for it offers hope, and go with it ...

Alicia referred to professionals who have given her support to make her own decisions for Juan Pablo, such as the on-site director at the child care center – "she's not there telling you what to do, but she's just thinking out loud … just somebody to listen and to process it" with you, calling them "my warriors on the ground." She spoke of the ways that suggestions from other parents when she was "ready to give up … for me, those were little miracles."

"You can't let life beat you down."

As she further articulated her thoughts about where she finds strength, she added:

> And sometimes you're tired, you want to sit down, you want to just forget about it! But there's always these little angels that come just in disguise of other parents or faculty members, teachers, and they sort of push you along without realizing it that that's what you needed at that time.

She added: "… and I guess this … inner strength comes from, I think also it's part of my experience of coming to this country as a refugee, it's linked to that." Making this connection, she said,

> Because we came with nothing and my parents, my father and my mother always were, "We had nothing but we came to this country to have something, and we have been given an opportunity and we need to take it." … and my mother was the pillar, she was the strength of that house …

She went on to talk about the ways her parents both worked to care for them, her mother always cooking delicious Cuban food and her father doing home improvements to keep the house in good repair. She contrasted their life to "the images we have of refugees coming to this country …" adding that their house was always warm and welcoming to others, including the neighbors, who would come to see what smelled so good: "… food was key … And very few people knew in this Gary, Indiana where we lived what Cuban food was." And she summed up beautifully what she learned growing up and what still guides her actions today in saying:

> So that strength of, okay, this is what we've been dealt, this is where we're at. We're not going to sit here and complain about it. We have to make the best out of it … you have to, you have to, you can't let life beat you down.

"I think that that belief in the higher power has also helped."

Alicia described herself as a Catholic now, although she was raised Episcopalian, and she talked about her sense of religion as integral to her life:

I think that that belief in the higher power has also helped … that's why I see meaning in what people may think are small, insignificant as we say, "details" or "detalles" in Spanish. For me, they're not small insignificant … there's like little angels with us sent by God or the higher power, how you want to call him, who's there to guide you.

She added:

… I believe in that strongly. And he wouldn't have given me this, I guess, if I couldn't deal with it. And there are days that I do feel, oh God! No. What now? But (pause) it's just pick up, you know, a minute, a second that happens, but then you just quickly pick up and you keep going because, and, and also, although autism is different from one kid to the other and you can't really compare kids on it, there are others who are worse off.

Alicia talked more about how challenging it was to finally become a parent after so many years of having a different kind of life: "… when I had Juan Pablo, it was really, it was a whole change. Even though you read and you think you understand what this is going to be all about, I was very naïve going into it …" Having watched her mother raise six children, she said:

… my father was busy and she was the one keeping us in order, and so she made it seem so easy, you know? So in my head, it was just, oh, it's easy! (laughs) We can do this. You know, we just give them the things. But never in my mind [did I] imagine that he, my son, would have a problem, an issue, a need. Never.

Alicia's mother, although she lived in Florida when Juan Pablo was born, was a great support to her. She and Juan Pablo made frequent visits to her mother because Alicia really wanted them to know each other. After his diagnosis of autism, Alicia shared "she would give me, as the Spanish would say, ánimo, encouragement …" When her mother would tell her, "no, that's not what he has–he's just fine, Alicia, don't worry about it" she still worried, but found her mother's words really helped her move forward. A moment of dialogue in our conversation illuminated the depth of her feelings for her mother, and how she still holds her in her heart:

INTERVIEWER: … it sounds like she was a great strength in your life too and you were very connected to her …
ALICIA: Yes. Yes, she was, she was, and she still is. I feel her. I feel her always near me … every time I … feel depressed or whatever, you know, she comes into my mind and helps me. "Okay, no, we gotta keep doing this."
INTERVIEWER: (overlapping) … and draw on her strength.
ALICIA: Exactly, exactly, definitely draw on her strength.

INTERVIEWER: Wow. So interesting. I didn't know all this stuff, so fascinating, you know. I knew your strength as a mother but now I see where it came from. (laughs)

ALICIA: It was really my mother.

"That's what I really want people to know, that he learns differently."

Alicia spoke about what she would like other people to understand about Juan Pablo:

> … this has come to me not because of an Aha! moment on its own, but from reading, observing, reflecting on it, that although he may have this diagnosis of autism, what that means really is that he has just a different way of learning … it's just a different way of learning that you need to be patient with, you need to understand, but that he can learn … and so, the rigor of the school shouldn't be less because he has this label.

She shared some of the ways that Juan Pablo continues to surprise her with what he knows, and that she does not think he learns it all at school. She talked about how he is using language that he has heard in the videos he watches on his iPad and generalizing it to new contexts and to his own personal experiences:

> … lately he's been using all kinds of terms and expressions, and I'm thinking to myself, my goodness, where is he getting that from? And although as educators we know we should and we need to limit the iPad and the iPhone and the IT stuff, I realize he's getting those phrases and he's using them in context because of that.

She also shared that there are some things he knows that are not reflected in his Individualized Educational Plan (IEP): "… he's counting backwards and front-wards, and he can count to a hundred, but the school only really acknowledges twenty. So when I get his IEPs, it's he can count up to twenty." She has noticed that he is beginning to recognize sight words related to some of his favorite books as well.

> And so that's why I have to step back, relax, breathe, and just say, Alicia, stop it. He learns differently, so it's not that he now needs to be put in some kind of fifty-thousand-dollar private independent school that will have him doing calculus when he's in first grade. You know, just (pause) but that's what I really want people to know, that he learns differently.

As the conversation continued, Alicia raised another issue that speaks to Juan Pablo's different ways of learning. As a university employee, she is entitled to some benefits to support her child's education, such as tuition reduction at a particular private school. However,

> ... none of that exists if you have a special ed child because [the University supported elementary school] doesn't really accept kids that have special needs ... Or learn (pause) in our sort of ... mainstream way of learning or how we think kids learn. So ... that's what I want people to know. They learn differently, but it's not, it shouldn't be taken as a negative or as something bad. It's just how are we going to better support kids like Juan Pablo.

"I had to learn how to learn so that I could be a better advocate to him, a better mother to him, a better support to him."

Asked what she had learned about herself through Juan Pablo, Alicia had an immediate response: "Oh my God! (laughs) Oh my God! Um (pause) you know, I don't say this, but that song comes to mind, 'I Will Survive' I will survive (singing) and not even will survive, but I can survive." She talked about learning the phrase "learning how to learn" while studying education in graduate school, but not fully understanding it then as she does now:

> ... and you know, I never really understood that expression (pause) ... But I—with Juan Pablo, I had to learn how to learn so that I could be a better advocate to him, a better mother to him, a better support to him.

Alicia shared her memories of her initial attitude toward some of the professionals working with Juan Pablo when he first began receiving services:

> And I remember ... when all of this started and he had all kinds of service providers going to our house, and sometimes, you know, you had like these high school-looking young providers coming to the house and I would sit there and say, "What nonsense is this, this silliness? What is happening here? It's like babysitting." And I had to get over ... that attitude. (pause) Peace, you know, just be quiet for a little bit. Observe. You know, be open to really hearing what they're doing and what they're saying, and seeing how it all was eventually coming together. So that (pause), that's one big thing ... he's taught me ... Just learning how to learn, be more reflective, be more just, I don't know how to put it, but being quiet. Quiet.

Alicia also talked about how she has learned to be more patient with Juan Pablo and to give him time to develop new skills. She reflected on how her father used to encourage her and her siblings to practice working with a pencil by making circles, something she is introducing to Juan Pablo to help strengthen his grip: "We didn't have coloring books, we didn't have toys, we were poor ... And we would do pages and pages and have fun and big ones and small ones ..."

Adding to this reflection, she said, "The other thing that he's helped me learn is that money is not everything. And that's important for me because, because I come from ... a financial needs background ..." She shared:

> And for me, one of the things that I thought was the solution to all your problems is throwing money at it. And so ... when he was first diagnosed and all these service providers started to come to my house ... when they left, I was immediately on Amazon ordering every single thing that I had seen them have ... And that's not the solution 'cause ... I am a creative person when I'm quiet and at peace. You know, you can find alternatives ... You have a box of Cheerios. Can you use that box of Cheerios to sort of do the same thing?

Alicia also paid for extra providers, to work with him, giving Juan Pablo perhaps more help than he really needed as she thinks back on that time.

> ... I realized, no, you know, I know why you're doing this. You feel that the more time and money you throw at this, the—no, no, no, you know what? Some of that stuff that hopefully you think they should be doing, you, me, mother and father, you can be doing at home because you're here to also teach ... some things. And as a parent, you have to be a partner in this process, and not just throwing money at babysitters and whoever else to do this for you.

"I want him to be a happy, well-adjusted child."

As our conversation moved toward Alicia's goals and dreams for Juan Pablo, it was clear from her response that her ideas on this topic are still evolving. She said, "I (sighs) you know, I have big goals, but (pause) lately this is becoming clearer for me. I want, I want him to be (pause) a happy (pause) well-adjusted child. That's it." In prioritizing this as her number one goal, Alicia has not forgotten about her dreams for Juan Pablo. She shares, "... yes, I want him to go to college, yes, I want him to get married. Yes, I want him to do this and that. But really, is he happy? Is he —well adjusted?"

Continuing in this vein, Alicia went on to describe the value in being happy with who you are.

> You're happy, that means you have friends. You're happy, it means you're happy at the school, you're doing well ... if you're happy, hopefully for me, it means also ... you have good self-esteem, you know ... you have a sense of security from your parents and from yourself. Well-adjusted means for me that you can really be anywhere at any place and be happy, be at peace, be content. (pause) That's it.

Alicia added one more element: "there's love, a loving child. He's very loving. He's always been very loving." Although she highly values Juan Pablo's loving nature, she says, "even still, that concerns me a little because he's just happy with people ... believes in them and ... I want him to realize, you know, that you need to be careful with that and all that."

"One of the basic things is knowing who my child is."

As Juan Pablo was approaching his transition to kindergarten, Alicia was once again busy looking for a new school for him. Asked what she thought professionals could do to help him achieve the goals she has for him, she said she felt that in his current school "*they have been* doing it ... they are able to be in tune with who he is, so really one of the basic things is knowing who my child is." She added: "that's why right now, as I think about kindergarten, you know, I've been trying to do everything possible to make sure that whatever kindergarten he goes to is a small kindergarten, where he has that individual attention, you know?"

Alicia returned again to the notion that Juan Pablo was a loving child, "*he's a very* loving, one on one type of person." She asked, "is that normal to expect when ... you get bigger and older, and out in the real world? You know what? I think yes ..." She went on to say that she thought that we are able to create a kinder reality for ourselves, "but you can't choose that reality if you don't know how it should feel or how it looks." She talked about the importance of a teacher's role in nurturing this knowledge while lamenting that "nowadays teachers ... are just not respected ... and yet ... we require so much from them, right?"

Summing up her feelings, she said,

> And so I hope ... that loving teacher really can focus on him as an individual and really encourage him ... by working with his strengths and seeing the strengths that he has, but letting him do what he wants within, you know, the framework. (pause) Being there for him.

"I was really at a loss."

I asked Alicia, "Tell me a little bit about what the initial process of accessing service and support was like for you as a parent, and how did you make decisions in that process?" She responded: "... I don't want to put this in a negative way. But if you're not (pause)—once I was able to get into EI intervention, things went very smoothly. But before then ... I was really at a loss." She talked about how her pediatrician was not really helpful when she began to have concerns about some of Juan Pablo's challenges with eating and sleeping: "she didn't really think he had an issue ..." Alicia added that the doctor didn't seem to know where to send her to get more information: "I don't want to blame her because in many other ways she's really great, but in retrospect I think ... why didn't she know?" She wondered why the pediatrician didn't have a list of referrals for her like the one we gave her at the center when Juan Pablo was 2 years old.

Alicia talked about the kinds of advice they were getting from people who thought "we are permissive … and if he doesn't want to go to sleep, you just lock him in the room and that's it, close the door. You know, all kinds of rubbish, to tell you the truth." She said, "You know, we, thank God we got it at two, but … I was ready for something at nine months. (laughs) … Something, and I didn't know, I just didn't know." Finally, after Alicia met with Juan Pablo's child care teachers and was given information about referral agencies, her pediatrician did give her a number to call, but

> … the number wasn't right, 'cause I remember calling and it was a long sort of process. I didn't know, because I didn't know where I was really trying to direct myself to. The operator didn't know where I needed to go to, and I just left that because of frustration. I just, what is, I couldn't even figure it out.

Once Alicia was able to connect with a responsive agency, she was surprised by how quickly and efficiently they responded.

> You know, they were willing to come? Really? The first time. They were willing to come to the house. They started the whole paperwork and the process, and that was days. I'm not saying a week or two. It was days.

She also had a smooth transition from EI to preschool, which she attributes to the support she received from one facilitator in particular who she didn't really trust at first.

> I would question her sometimes, and again, [she] looked like a little girl … but she's not a little girl. She had three kids of her own and … she was a professional, she knew how to do this. But we come to this with our bias of how these professionals need to look (laughs), even though we are dealing with those issues ourselves, you know? As a person of color, yes, you know, but (laughs) here was another, you know, another little angel that was sent to me so that I can learn something, and I was resisting the lessons initially.

She added that she only realized after the fact that this facilitator knew what was needed for a smoother transition from EI to preschool. She was being asked to sign certain forms that didn't make sense to her: "I didn't understand what she was talking about, but I finally decided, okay, I'm going to sign it, and voila! It was a smooth transition, there was no bump in the road, no gap in service at all."

"It's about where does he fit in his zone school."

At the time of our meeting, Alicia was beginning to gear up for what she had to do to negotiate Juan Pablo's next school placement. She had sought counsel from the university to see what kinds of financial support might be available for a private primary school. She was directed to a lecture on transition for children with special needs, where she recalled hearing:

> ... from the minute into early intervention and to even preK, it's a warm, fuzzy, you know, we love, we work together, we're a team, we're a community ... But when you start moving into the regular public school system, with kindergarten, you lose that ... They're not into what is the individual need of that child. It's about where does he fit in his zone school ...

Alicia talked about visiting her zone school, where she "realized this is not that fuzzy, warm, feeling ... for any kid. It's just (pause) well, this is where your apartment is, this is your zone school, and ... we think this is where you need to go." She said that this experience made her see that she would need help to negotiate for another school placement, anticipating a potential "adversarial relationship. It hasn't gotten there yet, but I've had to hire a lawyer."

She also

> ... had to dish out seven thousand dollars for a neuro-psych exam (pause) just to be ready because what's coming is not going to be warm and fuzzy. It's going to be this is it, this is what we can offer him, that's it. So ... since I need to really be an advocate for my son and demand not just (pause) special ed or whatever you have, but the best, for special needs kids, then I need to do all of this.

Alicia said she would be bringing her lawyer to the next transition meeting "Because ... I'm not going to—no, I'm not going to ramble." She hoped that bringing the lawyer would allow her to make clear demands because "we have the right to ..."

She talked more about how disappointed she was with the zone school program. She felt that the curriculum "wasn't rigorous enough" even though it was an inclusive classroom. She added:

> Even the kid that was playing on the computer sort of spelling words ... there was a para that was sitting with this group, and I wondered why isn't he helping that kid, you know, extending that lesson or something? And then my kid, Juan Pablo, one of his biggest issues is speech and language, so that it has to be a real rich language environment where he's not just repeating things or playing with an iPad ...

As an alternative to the zone school, Alicia had been visiting private special education schools, but found that most of them were prohibitively expensive, saying: "All of them are in that price range, forty-five to fifty thousand dollars a year." She later added:

... where's the support for us? ... I know of other parents that are ... scrambling around and doing their own thing, and you know, they may have their own funding ... but even if you do have the funding, there should be a support because you're paying taxes like everybody else.

Alicia said that going through this process made her see that

you have to do this, this is—it's not just me, but it's other parents ... so many parents are doing this. You have to hire the lawyer and you have to do the neuro-psych ... what I feel is if you don't do it, then your kid will be sitting there. They'll accept him for kindergarten, but because ... they're not giving them the individual support that they need, so he's not going to pass the first grade and he's going to be repeating first grade, or ... to put it on the flip side, they'll pass him, but he's a first grader in a kindergarten class still learning the letter sounds. My kid knows the letter sounds.

"But we're there with him."

Listening to Alicia talk about a typical day in their family life, I was reminded of how much energy she has put into thinking about both Juan Pablo's needs and how to best create an atmosphere at home that supports who they are as a family. As she implied in various parts of our conversation, getting to where they are now has been a journey with many stops and turns along the way. What follows is a thumbnail sketch of a day in the life of Alicia, Juan Pablo, and his father.

I wake up at six-thirty and I get dressed ... then I wake him up around seven ... seven-ten the latest. I have everything laid out already. Even lunch is already made. And I dress him while he's sleeping. He doesn't wake up ... if I want to have him out the door by seven-thirty, I do what I need to do ... we need to literally walk a block and, and the bus is there basically ... but he won't walk, so my husband ... he's, you know, getting his act together ... so what he does is he gives him a horsey ride ... if I break that routine, if I make something different, it's when I see that he gets distracted.

Juan Pablo attends school until 2:00 pm. He takes the bus home and either Alicia or her husband "has to be at home to pick him up."

Because I'm putting money into all the other stuff, I need to focus on what I need, and so we just alternate between who picks him up. So that means that, for example, after I finish here, I'll go home and I'll pick him up ... and then ... he will either want to go to McDonald's (pause) for chicken nuggets or he'll want to have pizza ...

Alicia says:

> even though I have pizza, homemade pizza in the refrigerator that I can put in the microwave and it's really great, or I even have chicken nuggets … I think I've learned that it's his way of connecting with us and he likes, he sees that we take him to, you know, wherever we take him, we sit there with him, and he'll eat and he'll ask for his iPad or his You Tube, so we usually give it to him. But we're there with him, I'll ask him about the day and he's saying um, you know, birthday today or a student's name, and so that's part of the process.

She adds: "… do I really want to go home now, pick him up, and go to McDonald's? NO! … but I need to do it."

Once they arrive at home, Juan Pablo spends time on his iPad and playing with his toys independently. After an hour or two, he goes to find Alicia: "… he'll come to my room and he'll say, 'Shut down the computer, shut down the computer.' He'll tell me that." Alicia keeps a special bag of toys in her closet full of things they do together, such as painting or puzzles, which Juan Pablo will specifically ask for. After this special shared playing time, Alicia makes Juan Pablo some biscuits that he especially likes for dinner. In a brief moment of dialogue, she shares:

ALICIA: He doesn't eat anything else that I will cook. He'll have the biscuits. So at least I'm giving him—
INTERVIEWER: So that allows you to also do that thing you want to do, like your mother. (laughs)
ALICIA: (overlapping) Exactly.
INTERVIEWER: You cook something, you feed him
ALICIA: You feed him and he'll eat it, which is like it brings joy.
INTERVIEWER: Yes!

While Juan Pablo is eating his biscuits, Alicia starts the preparations for the following day. She washes dishes and makes his lunch. He has long been a very picky eater, and his occupational therapist is working on this with him. Alicia packs a vegetable for this purpose: "he has to at least smell it, hold it in his mouth for like five seconds … but then he spits it back out." Around 8:30 or 9:00 pm he takes a bath. This is a ritual that he does with his father. After the bath, he spends more time playing with games; Alicia does not allow the iPad after the bath.

> … at around ten o'clock, max, is when I will come to him with my timer. I have a timer and I'll say ten minutes, fifteen minutes, what do you want? But no more. You can have five, ten, fifteen minutes to close down and get ready for bed. And … he'll protest, he'll always say, Five, ten, fifteen or whatever. It's never that; he'll want more.

When it is finally time for bed, "… we go to the room, the room where he sleeps, and that's where, even if I don't want to, which I never really want to, I need to get in bed with him."

They read a few of his favorite books, and "by ten-thirty, he's asleep." She adds: "but that's when he's on schedule. If anything weird happens, he can be up at eleven, eleven-thirty, and just, you know, running around and we're trying to quiet him down …"

"Mommy, I love you."

"What would you say is the most enjoyable part of that day for you?" I asked. Alicia replied:

> … he's always, as you know, been a very loving child, and so for example, yesterday, Sunday, we had a really lovely day without any tantrums, nothing. I took him outside, nothing special. Went to the park … I had him run because he loves to run, so we were running, he was running after me. And you know, for me, the best part of that day or any day is in the evening, he said, 'Mommy, I love you.'

She continued to describe Juan Pablo as "a kid that just, you know, exudes love" and even though he may not say it every day, she says, "That makes it all (pause) worth it."

Alicia described herself as the disciplinarian in the family, as she is the one who sets limits and reinforces the routines. She shares:

> You know, we, we have a routine here, even though it may seem that we don't, but we do have a routine. And my husband doesn't believe in any routine at all, and just give him whatever, or you know, give him, give him the iPad to sleep. NO!

But she also added that she does give in to Juan Pablo at times. He can be very persistent.

"The dining room table is becoming a place of coming together."

Asked about special times they share or celebrate as a family, Alicia talked first about her love of travel:

> I'm a traveler, I love traveling, and that is something that I feel I do share as a family. But it's, it's with him (Juan Pablo). It's not really with my husband because my husband can be quite difficult with traveling.

However, she added that her husband "is beginning to see the benefits of all this that we're doing together, and I must say that … finally my husband is onto the program that we need to eat together as a family." She talked again about not being raised that way, but said she can see that it makes a difference for Juan Pablo: "… he needs to see me sitting at that table and, and that's the family time." She shared that they had previously allowed Juan Pablo to develop some bad eating habits:

> We don't do this, but we allowed it, I allowed it for him to go to the bedroom and eat on the bed. Until one day I was just fed up! Because I was washing sheets every day because … he still loves chocolate, there's chocolate all over. Enough! (claps hands) What you needed to learn when you were two years old, you're going to learn now, and he did. And so we sit at the table … the dining room table is becoming a place of coming together.

"But they do have a very, very special bond."

When I asked Alicia, "And would you say that your husband has any special things that he does with him?" she responded, "… they do have a very, very special bond. My son adores his father because the father is the good cop." She shared an anecdote about how Juan Pablo ran into his father's office and locked the door so she couldn't get in. She tried to lure him out by playing a game of the Three Little Pigs. "Open up! Open up! You know, little pig, little pig, open the door! (laughs) And then he'll say, Not by the rrrrr that I'm the wolf. I am the wolf. I have to blow, you know?" But even this game that usually entices him was not enough to get him to leave his father's side. She added:

> They're in that room together often … sometimes when I take him out, I have to tell my husband to leave, to take a walk, to go to Starbuck's because if my husband is there, he won't want to do it.

Alicia talked a little more about the different dynamics in her versus her husband's relationship with Juan Pablo. With her, she says, "… it's a constant sort of lesson when we do anything together, which he gets tired of." With her husband, "… it's easier (pause) none of this. You know? … he can just do I guess boy things … They kick back and do whatever. So he has different relationships with both."

As Alicia is coming to accept these differences in parenting styles between her and her husband, she also reflected on the importance to Juan Pablo of the relationship dynamics between the two of them. She shared, "I mean, you know, he's four years old, dealing with his own challenges, but I really—he understands, I mean, the dynamics in the house haven't always been that good. Now it's quiet and peaceful. (knocks table)" She added: "… in some families, a divorce would have been on the table a long time ago, but it's the son that has really kept us together." Alicia's final words in response to this question: "That's something I've had to learn, you know? To each his own and he does love him in a different way."

"... to tell the story and talk about it with somebody without feeling judged."

Asked about sharing any advice that has been particularly helpful to her, Alicia went back to something she said earlier: "... you need to be the one that needs to be celebrating and applauding your efforts. (pause) That's it. Nobody else is going to do that." Adding to this notion, she shared:

> ... that has kept me going when I'm really feeling like why am I doing all this running around? Drained! ... and why are you doing this? Your son. Keeping him at the center and knowing that, you know, it's the most thankless job. And if you haven't really learned how to do that, get into it. Do some yoga, some Zen Buddhism (laughs), whatever you need ... just internally thank yourself for this and be content with that because that's all you're gonna get! (claps)

Asked if there was anything else she wanted to share before ending our conversation, Alicia offered a lovely anecdote about Juan Pablo.

> ... one little thing we have, I mean, psychology-wise, I don't know if this is right or wrong, but he came up with it and he said to me, "You're my queen and I'm the king." He was learning about kings and queens and unicorns and I don't know, but now he says, I'm his queen. I've taken it now and have sort of made it my own little thing, but I keep remembering that when I thank myself for what I'm doing. Really not even just for him, but for our, for us ... The family, you know?

In closing, we thanked each other for this precious time we spent together. Alicia said:

> It's the educational community and the people in it who have been my greatest support, and this is ... a source of support as well 'cause I'm able to tell the story and talk about it with somebody without feeling judged, without feeling, you know, all kinds of negative things because there's people out there that are your friends but they don't really understand it.

Questions for Discussion

1. How would you describe Alicia's family strengths and resources?
2. How does Alicia's family work together to support their child and each other?
3. How would you characterize Alicia's communication and collaboration with professionals?

4. Throughout her story, Alicia expresses uncertainty about Juan Pablo's diagnosis. How can professionals value a family's questioning and encourage them to maintain a hopeful outlook regarding their child's potential?

5. In this story, we hear a parent struggle with trusting others and feeling judged. Can you think of a time that you have felt judged by others? What strategies helped you navigate these feelings and access the support you needed?

4

A FAMILY REFLECTS ON THE CHALLENGES AND ACHIEVEMENTS IN THEIR DAILY LIVES

Helen and Ben Foster agreed to meet for their interview in a local café. The setting wasn't ideal – it was a little noisy and the café was scheduled to close in less than an hour – but all agreed to start the conversation and see how it would go. Once underway, Helen usually took the lead in answering questions, but Ben also offered his own quiet and thoughtful perspectives from time to time. Fortunately, the restaurant staff generously let the meeting continue even though it extended 45 minutes after their official closing time.

At the start of the conversation, both Helen, 44 and Ben, 45 identified themselves as African American. Helen described the members of their family: "Well, we have three kids. An adult daughter with no issues, Elisa, she's nineteen years old. And we also have Joshua, he's thirteen, and Sienna, who is ten."

"Mainly they lend an ear."

When asked about other important people in their lives, Helen added:

> I have a friend across the street and she also has a son that is also on the spectrum that's three years old, and (pause) I have my father-in-law, the children's grandfather, and (pause) my, my family, but they live a ways away.

When Ben was asked the same question, he replied: "My father. (pause) My in-laws, and (pause) that's basically it." Helen and Ben described the ways that these people in their lives offered support; Helen said: "Mainly they lend an ear, they're there to listen (pause) basically that's it," while Ben added:

My father sometimes, if we're short on money for the kids, he'll help out with that and my in-laws will once in a while send some clothing … And whenever we have problems, we can call them up and they can give us advice about whatever if we don't know anything.

"It's just that I just realized that I didn't have a little baby anymore."

As the conversation continued, Ben and Helen were asked if they could think of an example of a recent time that they had received this kind of help or advice. Helen jumped in with an interesting set of anecdotes that quickly moved our conversation to the next level. She said: "Well, Sienna just started menstruating." When asked how old Sienna was she replied: "Ten! She just started menstruating so I was crazy so I called everyone." Asked what kind of advice she got, Helen shared:

A lot of it was not useful advice. But it was concerned advice, you know what I mean? So, it was things like, 'Oh, maybe you better put her on birth control. Are you worried about someone bothering her sexually?', things like that. I wanted things like, 'Oh, just keep her routine going.' Like I got that more from like the therapist and the BA (Behavior Analyst). But from family, I got mainly, 'Oh my goodness, she's ten years old. Now you have to worry about people trying to sexually harass her.'

Helen spoke to some of her concerns about navigating this new aspect of parenting with her daughter.

So yeah, and then you have to worry about cramps and, and her changing, keeping clean. And (pause) so they would say things like, you know, maybe giving her birth control or looking into whether they do a hysterectomy on someone that young for their period. Those are things at ten years old I don't even want to consider any of that.

Asked which advice was helpful to her, Helen paused and had to think for a moment. She shared:

… the therapist was more helpful, where she was just telling me, oh, just, you know, because all along I've been trying to show Sienna like, you know, how to change herself and things like that. So just basically the therapist telling me, you know, just to keep repetition.

Asked how the conversation went with Sienna, Helen replied: "It went right over her head (laughs) It went right over her head. So, I tried to make a deal of it." She continued to describe what happened on that eventful day:

Oh wow. They called me from her school and they told me, they sent me a text. "Sienna just started menstruating." I was like, oh my goodness. I knew it was coming ... But I, I—it's still a surprise. So (pause) that day, me and Benny, we went to a Walgreens and I bought all the little stuff. I wanted to make it special. Maxi-Pads, feminine cleanser wipes, a little thing of Advil, and some chocolate. (laughs) So you know, things like that to make it a little special. But Sienna I don't think was fazed by it in the least, you know? She didn't get cramps or anything so she just kind of—I asked her what happened when she got home. She's like, I got my period, and then she went back to going on her tablet or whatever ... it wasn't a big deal to her but it was a huge deal. (laughs)

Asked how he felt about this milestone as Sienna's father, Ben responded: "Well, I don't know if it's a milestone. It's just that I just realized that I didn't have a little baby anymore."

"He's doing some things he's not supposed to do."

Asked about particular challenges that Josh and Sienna might be facing at this stage in their lives, Helen talked more about parenting them through puberty. Although she was reluctant to say the word, her indications were clear as she discussed Josh's new habit of masturbating.

Yeah. Josh—it's mainly regular things, like with a teenage boy, so he's starting to sprout some hair on his chin. He's doing some things he's not supposed to do. Like luckily he stopped doing it as much ... I don't know if I'm supposed to say that one, but yeah.

She talked about a strategy that she learned from his teacher, which seems to be helping: "I've just learned, like his teacher uses (pause) 'it's inappropriate,' so I only said that a few times and he understands now that he's not supposed to, or he's supposed to go to a private place and do that."

Helen also talked about some challenging changes in Sienna's behavior, sharing: "And then the attitude, the hormones and the attitude kicking in. I can't get my way and the crying because I can't get my way, you know?" Ben began to share a story about the family's recent trip to Barnes and Noble: "We went to Barnes and Noble's just to look around at some books. Sienna wanted a book very, very bad. And we were getting ready to leave and we told her—I don't know if she acted up while she was in the store." Helen chimed in to clarify the details: "So we were in the store. This is a trip that was a week in the making. She's been asking that whole week, 'I wanna go to Barnes and Noble's, wanna go to Barnes and Noble's.'" Helen continued to describe how Sienna reacted when she was told she could only have one book:

... so we're looking around the children's department. I kind of just let them, set them free in the children's department. She comes back with a handful of books, like this, she's got her hands crossed over the books. And I tell her, 'No, you can only have one.' And she makes a beeline for the door of the store ... I was maybe a week or two out of my surgery, so Elisa's right behind her. So, she gets the books from her. She (pause) I guess she puts them back or whatever, and then Sienna goes and collects the books again. Makes a beeline for the door. This time Dad catches her ... (laughs) Yeah, this time Dad catches her and he puts the books back, and now, now he's dragging her out of the store. 'I WANNA BOOK! I WANNA BOOK!' So how embarrassing. Now she's in the corridor of the Mall (laughs) and she's screaming, 'I WANNA BOOK! I WANNA BOOK! WHY WON'T YOU GET ME A BOOK!' And people are looking at her.

Asked, "Can you think of what you'd want people to know or understand at that moment?" Helen responded:

At that moment, I kind of wanted them just to, you know, stop like frowning up because at this time, I'm angry, so I take her by her arm and I'm taking her to the elevator because I'm going to take her upstairs to the bathroom so we can talk about this, you know? ...

So, people are looking and they're frowned up and they're doing this. Some of them got their camera phone out ... And, so I find myself usually in those situations when people are looking like that, I'm saying, SHE'S AUTISTIC! You know, hoping that people understand, you know? Hoping that people understand this is why this big girl with breasts that's as tall as I am is kicking, and screaming on the floor, you know?

As the conversation continued, Ben discussed his concern that Sienna is spending too much time on her tablet, and Helen added her insight:

BEN: I don't think Sienna listens, well she's in her own world because she's so entrenched in her tablet, and when you try to say something to her, and she's not listening at all. And I always felt she's too wrapped up and into it

HELEN: I think – and I don't want to speak for you, but sometimes I think he finds it hard to make a connection with her because of the tablet.

Both parents agreed that the tablet does get in the way of connecting with Sienna. They also have concerns about what she is watching on it at times, as Helen described:

HELEN: ... when she gets home, before we're even in the door good, she gets that tablet and turns it on. So (pause) getting it from her, taking it from her so you can talk to her was the only way to get her to respond. So, I usually end up taking it from her if I need her to do something and pay attention to me.

INTERVIEWER: What does she like to do on the tablet?

HELEN: It's usually You Tube and (pause) it's maybe My Little Pony or the Fresh
Beats Band, but I think it's maybe a meme that someone else might have –
like not a meme but a, like somebody might have rearranged it where it's
got like adult content in it, you know? So maybe it's the My Little Pony
drinking whiskey or some, or something like that, or chopping each other's head
off and, I don't know how to – you know and things like that, so I don't know,
somebody takes those cartoons and they make it bad. (laughs)

INTERVIEWER: And Ben, you feel like sometimes the tablet gets in the way?

BEN: Yeah, what I was saying, 'good morning' she would just look and see the
tablet and 'How you doing?' And then, well I would have to just threaten to
just cut off the Wi-Fi and then I'll get a response from her.

Ben and Helen described the ways that the children respond differently to their
parenting styles. Both see Ben as more of the authority figure. Using the example
of getting Josh up in the morning, Helen said with her, "it takes a full twenty
minutes before he's finally out of the bed" but with Ben "he doesn't have to say
nothing. He comes and stands in the door of his (Josh's) room and he'll get up.
(laughs) But for me, it takes twenty minutes."

"They're making me proud every day."

As the conversation turned to things that are going well, Helen and Ben had
much to share. They talked about the ways that their son "Josh's behavior has
changed tremendously." Helen discussed the ways he "used to do a lot of
screaming" in response to trigger sounds, like a dog barking or a baby crying.
With help from his therapists, Josh was able to become desensitized to these
sounds so that he can better cope with them. She described how her friend's
3-year-old's behavior no longer is as irritating to Josh: "he whines constantly
and it doesn't bother Josh like it used to … You know, actually Josh kind of
laughs at it." She also talked about Sienna's progress: "Oh my goodness, she's
curious" (laughs), and how grown up their older daughter has become: "Oh, and
Elisa is an adult." Helen added: "I'm proud of all of them, you know, they're
making me proud every day." Ben responded: "Elisa is successful in college right
now. Josh is improving in his school. Sienna is about to graduate this year from
elementary school."

"We have our own way of communicating to each other."

Helen and Ben shared what they see as some of their family's strengths, starting
with their ways of being there for each other. Ben clarified this by saying: "It's
almost like, you know, if one is sick, like everybody will go to him to check on

him and see if he's okay." Helen elaborated on this by sharing the ways the whole family helped when she recently had a hysterectomy:

> I think Josh knew—that he could sense, you know, there was something wrong. Benny would tell him Mommy's in the hospital, so when I called him from the hospital, he knew where I was and they knew something was wrong and that was my fear, that I had stomach surgery and they would be trying to jump on me. But no, they kind of knew and they were kind of like easy and gentle with me, especially around my stomach, Sienna would pat and rub it all the time.

Ben added that their older daughter, Elisa, "was a huge help you know, with Sienna and Josh."

"We're in defense of each other."

As the discussion continued, Helen and Ben described some difficult experiences they have encountered with the children in public places, and the ways they have bonded together as a family in responding to these incidents. Helen stated: "… if someone says something wrong or does something wrong we're all like, hey! No! Don't do that, you know?" Asked for a clarifying example, Helen told the story of a time the whole family had gone to dinner at TGI Fridays several years earlier:

HELEN: So, we went to Friday's, took the kids out for dinner … Josh was probably six or seven, Sienna was probably maybe around three or four … Elisa was probably just starting her teens, maybe thirteen, fourteen … and there's a lady, she's maybe drunk or belligerent or whatever, and she's saying, 'Hey, shut those kids up!' You know, Josh has a lot going on, the noise was bothering him … he got himself into a high chair when he was too big for it and he got stuck in it, so he was crying. Josh was making a lot of noise. No one else in the restaurant seemed to be bothered by it, but this lady came and made everything worse. 'Shut that kid up! Take him outside!' … I'm trying to explain to her 'He's autistic, I'm very sorry.' 'I don't care!' Blah blah blah blah.

INTERVIEWER: How did you feel when that was happening?

HELEN: It was, it was horrible. I mean I wanted to cry in front of her but I found the strength to hold it back. (laughs)

INTERVIEWER: Do you remember how you felt when that was happening, Ben?

BEN: I felt angry that − she upset my family and my wife.

HELEN: He even had some words for her, you know. It was like, 'Look, if you don't like it, you can leave' … Luckily the manager came in and got rid of her … I thought I was on an episode of "What Would You Do?"

"I have a voice now."

Although Helen ended up feeling good about the way the manager handled things, she reflected on what a different place she is in now as compared to back then:

> I didn't have a backbone then and I didn't have a voice then. Today, if that was to happen, I have a voice now. I'm an advocate now. I think I would be able to defend my children and myself better. I probably would have got thrown out of the restaurant. I would have been having an argument back and forth. If I wanted to, I didn't want to do that in front of the kids, but I feel like I would have handled it differently today. And it might not have been pretty. (laughs)

Ben added:

> If I would have handled it today, if it would have happened the same, I would just, just been calm and just asked for a manager and explain to the manager what was going on and let the manager take care of it instead of just—yeah.

"They're people just like you are."

The conversation flowed very naturally toward another of the interview questions, as Helen and Ben were asked, "What would you like other people to understand about your children?" They both had important things to say; Helen spoke first: "I want them to understand that they're people too. They're not sick. You don't have to be sorry when I tell you that they're autistic. They're people just like you are. They laugh, they enjoy music" She said that she thought other people saw the children as … "lower than them or (pause) not the same, somehow not the same … they don't treat them with the respect that they would someone else." Helen went on to describe how sometimes the people that work with Josh and Sienna lose patience with them and yell at them. She said she realized that it was easy to do that and she had done it herself sometimes too, especially with Sienna:

> … along with having autism, she has ADHD, so there's a lot of times, you're saying, 'Sienna, Sienna, Sienna, Sienna.' Then finally, 'SIENNA!' And that's the one that gets her attention, you know? So, I don't want to say I see her as not a person, but I know it's easy to lose your temper, you know what I'm saying? … And you know, it's kind of easy to lose your temper because you're constantly calling her and she's not answering, and you're thinking, well, what's wrong? You should be answering. I know you hear me. I'm sitting right next to you. Mmm.

But both she and Ben wanted people interacting with Josh and Sienna to have more patience. Helen said: "Have some patience because maybe they're not going to understand it as quick as you do." Ben added:

> Josh and Sienna are just like everybody else. They just have different ways of communicating, different ways of moving around and understanding stuff. And I just learn myself if you're patient with them and you just give them time to respond and understand, they'll respond to it.

"They're stepping into their excellence."

As the conversation moved toward the things that Helen and Ben feel good about as parents, both had important things to share. Helen's response focused on supporting the children's special interests: "I feel really good that my kids are turning into what they're supposed to be. They're stepping into their excellence, you know?" Asked to elaborate, she continued:

> Yeah. So, Elisa, I can see that she's going to be something big one day and she's focused and she's going somewhere—And Sienna, she loves to sing, you know? And I can see stuff starting to mold in this. We went to the National Night Out celebrations all over [our area]. They had a singing contest. She didn't ask me, 'Mommy, can I sing?' Before I knew it, she was up on the stage singing. And Josh, he loves his cars. And I can have—he's just gotten to the point maybe in the last couple of weeks where I can have a back-and-forth conversation with him. If I ask him something, he'll answer my question. So, they're stepping into who they're supposed to be, and it's normal, it's not handicapped and it's not autistic. It's normal, you know?

Ben talked more about them staying out of trouble:

BEN: Elisa is not acting like some kids or some teens and being irresponsible and stuff like that. That she's focused on getting herself better and stuff like that.

HELEN: A lot of kids where we come from, teenagers, girls Elisa's age are probably pregnant or have children by now. And it just makes me very proud to see that she wants to make her life first before she embarks on all that other stuff, you know? It makes me feel like I did something right, keeping this hold on her like I did.

BEN: I taught Elisa early about what you're not to do. I told her get pregnant before seventeen or eighteen, it's gonna be your responsibility to take care of it. And I also told her to get your financial stuff ready before you start a family …

When asked specifically about Josh and Sienna, both parents talked more about discipline.

HELEN: With me, I was trying – I'm not as lenient as I used to be. If you cry enough, it used to be like, oh, okay, come on, let's do it. I feel like I'm getting a little bit more of a backbone now as far as that.

BEN: I'm strict with them. All of the time I mean, if it was up to me, they wouldn't get away with half the stuff they get away with now because they know also that I only have to say stuff one time

HELEN: Yeah, he's more of the disciplinarian. Me, I don't like to see them cry, you know? (laughs)

When asked what they have learned about themselves through their children, Helen said, "I didn't know I had so much patience. I thought I was short of patience." Ben shared that he was also "learning how to understand kids with special needs more."

"I want them to be as normal as possible."

Helen and Ben described their goals and dreams for Josh and Sienna, each from their own perspective. Helen emphasized their ability to live more independently, saying she hoped they would be:

> Normal, normal as possible would be maybe one day having an apartment, even if it's assisted living. You know, being able to have a normal life. I want Sienna to have a boyfriend. I want Josh to have a girlfriend if that's what they want. I want them to work a job. I want them (pause) to be their normal, quote-unquote.

Ben said: "Just to be productive citizens. It means hold down a job, take care of their family if they have one, and not get in trouble or arrested."

As the conversation continued, Helen and Ben shared some of the ways that professionals are helping to support these goals. Helen offered the example of helping Sienna to learn the value of money:

> I want Sienna to learn the value of money. I called her therapist about that to enforce that at home, to show me how to enforce that at home … So, we're making a chart and it'll be chores. Sienna will earn fifty cents for making a bed, fifty cents for cleaning the table off, fifty cents for cleaning the floor, and (pause) so she gets that immediately, she gets that money immediately so she can see, okay, this is fifty cents and it's going into my piggy bank. And every fifty cents I collect is going to turn into a dollar and then five dollars and ten dollars, whatever. So, it's teaching her not only the value of money but how to save money and, and how to have a work ethic.

Ben emphasized the importance of professionals doing their job, saying: "just extend yourself above and beyond their job description."

"It's a big stack of paperwork."

When Helen and Ben were asked about their initial process in accessing services for their children Helen shared: "… so initially accessing these services was kind of hard because it's daunting, it's a lot of paperwork, it's a big stack of paperwork." She explained how she had some concerns about Josh when he was around 2 years old:

HELEN: We knew there was a problem with him from about two years old. We knew that there was something different. Couldn't put our finger on it, then we saw maybe a commercial on TV, it was about autism. We asked the pediatrician. She's like, 'Naw, he's a boy. These things happen.'

INTERVIEWER: What kinds of things were you noticing, do you remember?

HELEN: He was doing things like lining shoes up, he was doing the toe walking and the hands flapping. And (pause) things like that. And (pause) the pediatrician at that time told me, 'You know, boys are slower, these are things that boys do.' And (pause) so as time went on, Josh maybe had – did he have any speech? He had a little speech when he first started, right?

BEN: Yeah. A little bit.

HELEN: Yeah, and, and he went from having that little bit of speech to not having any speech at all.

INTERVIEWER: How old was he?

HELEN: He was around three when I noticed it. (pause) Around three. And it was around then that they could start preschool, and I knew there was a problem with him. So, I wrote the initial letter to the Board of Education to have him diagnosed, like from the beginning of the school year, but that was … like a half a year process.

INTERVIEWER: Just to be evaluated?

HELEN: Just to be evaluated. (laughs) I wrote the letter like maybe the first day of school to the special education department. He didn't get into an autism contained class until February of that school year. And (pause) Sienna didn't get in (interruption) Sienna didn't get into a program. When she started preschool, it took a whole year just for her to get into an autism contained program. Then they both went to [a different school] and they've had – and I have to say they have had, once they got there, a great teacher. Teachers that were invested in their job. But with Josh, it got to a point where it was all too much when those bells ringing and noises he wasn't used to, and homework and a lot of overwhelming things that played into him. He also had an abusive teacher's aide.

INTERVIEWER: Hmm, what was that like?

HELEN: … at that time, I couldn't – understand what he was saying. It was like, 'Mr. M., Mr. M, sit your ass down!' That's what Mr. M. would tell him. And Mr. M. would pluck him in the head with his fingers.

INTERVIEWER: He was the teacher?

HELEN: He was an aide. An aide or a one to one to someone else in the class-room, but he would take it on himself to handle Josh, you know? He wasn't Josh's one on one.

INTERVIEWER: And you learned about this from Josh?

HELEN: From Josh. He would say these things over and over. But then another parent came to me and told me, 'Is Mr. M. saying things, or is your kid saying stuff about Mr. M.?' And we ended up going to the Board of Ed about this situation.

INTERVIEWER: And how did that unfold?

HELEN: He ended up retiring out. They gave him the opportunity to retire out and there was talk, I remember there being talk of him being fired, there was talk, all kinds of talk, but then what I finally heard was he took the option to retire. Mmm.

"God is not that cruel."

The process of accessing services for Sienna was different, as Helen shared:

> I didn't really notice things about Sienna. I didn't take it that she was autis-tic … I thought it was her imitating Josh, you know, 'cause how could God possibly do that to me, you know? How could God possibly do that to us? Both of, both my kids are autistic. So I thought she's imitating Josh.

Helen described how one of Josh's teachers told her one day "Mom, she's autistic too. You better go have her checked." Sienna at this time was going on 4 years old. Helen was still not convinced: "I was like, okay, I'll have her checked out, but it ain't nothing, she ain't doing nothing but imitating Josh. And just like, man, God, God is not that cruel. He couldn't, he couldn't do that twice, you know?" When she got the diagnosis of autism, she said "I don't think it registered with me when they diagnosed her … It was years later that it probably registered … When I started seeing real behaviors from her."

"It's been a blessing."

Asked whether she still thought about those feelings – that God could not do this twice – Helen responded:

> No, because they're so normal now. It looks normal to me, you know? So, it's not, it's not, oh my God, kind of thing … a couple weeks ago … my girl-friend's husband was telling me how he sat and cried when his son was diag-nosed … You know, I have a brother that's autistic … so it didn't really register with me, so when people were like, 'Oh, I cried when I found out he was autistic,' I don't think I felt any of that. I felt some of that way later when

I was in it, you know? Like when I was in the throes of it, not somebody telling me it's happening. When somebody was telling me (pause) you know, like, oh, Sienna's pulling fire alarms at school … That's when it got upsetting.

Ben remembered that at these stressful times, he did sometimes ask: "Why did it happen to me or why did it happen to us? … Was the purpose of why it's happening to us that maybe it's happening to teach us something or to guide us in a different work?"

When asked, "Do you think it has taught you something?" Helen responded: "I think we were too busy to, we were too busy with the both of them to realize, to sit down and feel sorry for ourselves, you know? We didn't have a chance." Ben added that it has taught him to "be more compassionate; that everything happens for a reason." As Helen and Ben continued to reflect on this, Helen, in particular, talked about the children in a different way:

And it has, it's been a blessing. Two really loving kids. They are so sweet, the both of them, and they're always saying something cute, you know? (pause) And Josh is just a teddy bear. For such a big boy, he's a teddy bear, and that's—people, a lot of people are scared 'cause he's such a big guy.

"What would I want my mother to do for me?"

Describing some of their goals for the children and what principles guide their thinking as they help navigate the children's future, Helen responded: "If it was me, what would I want my mother to do for me?" As they talked about the transitions that will be coming up for Josh and Sienna in several years, Helen shared her ambivalence about having them grow up and become more independent:

You know, after taking care of people for the last thirteen years or for nineteen years … I was thinking, oh my goodness, I'm gonna have to take care of them for the rest of my life. [But] I may not because they are so much closer to normal, or what people perceive as normal.

Ben added that he wanted: "to have Josh and Sienna have a better life than what we lived up to this point. To do better than us. Financially, spiritually, mentally, all that, all around." Asked to clarify what he meant by "spiritually" Ben replied: "to have them have a stronger belief in God."

Helen agreed that she wanted her children to have more faith,

'cause sometimes I lose my faith, especially when something's happening; 'cause it's always something. If you're not fighting with the school district to get them what they need, you're fighting with the insurance company because we're going to cut you off, you know?

She and Ben talked about some ways that they work to instill faith in their children. Helen said: "When I can. When I remember, I try. I pray every night, but sometimes I forget to put Sienna and Josh on their knees to pray, you know?" Ben said: "Just by reassuring them." They do try to take the children to church, but sometimes it is difficult because "it's just too loud." They talked about some of the other things they do as a family, like going out to eat or taking day trips to the beach or to the city. They see these experiences in part as opportunities for the children to learn "to cope with all that's going on around [them]." Helen shared that she has recently started taking Sienna to get her hair and her nails done, and Ben goes with Josh to the barber shop.

"I like consistency with my people."

As the conversation moved toward the topic of communication with professionals, Ben had a short but clear response: "Just on my end, it's all about me trusting them." Helen reiterated this feeling, but also had a little more to say:

> I like consistency with my people ... Josh has a male therapist (Nick). Sienna has Monique, a female therapist. They're like a part of the family now. I love that Nick doesn't mind to push the Cheerios to the side that Josh has put all over the floor and sit down on the floor and play with him, you know?

Helen described how she felt comfortable with these therapists: "I felt safe talking to them; I didn't feel like [they] were judging me." She talked about the ways that Monique does special things with Josh too, and how much she trusts her:

> Josh likes to play with her shoes for some reason. (laughs) She wears cool shoes, so Josh wants to try them on. Josh comes and she'll take off her shoes and let him try them on. (laughs) And you know, I feel like (pause) if I were to die tomorrow, I would be all right with Monique raising her (Sienna). Although I know she can't do that, but I feel that way.

Helen also talked about another specialist who works with Josh who is not so consistent, emphasizing the importance of clear communication: "So, if I tell him, look, you either gotta call me if you're not coming or something, he tries to go by that." She added: "He's not very consistent. But now you've been with Josh a year, so I can't say, well, okay, I want somebody else, 'cause now Josh has gotta get used to a new person. So who am I hurting, right?"

"No matter what I put these people through, they still loved me."

Asked what she would like her children to remember about their educational experiences Helen had this to say: "That people loved me. These people, no matter what I was going through, they still loved me, no matter what I put them through." Ben's response echoed his strong sense of responsibility shared earlier in the conversation: "I don't want them to look back and, you know, on somebody's therapist couch talking about how we messed up their lives ... That we did the best for them as far as their lives are concerned."

As the discussion drifted into describing a typical day for the Foster family, Helen shared the daily routines of getting ready for school, including Sienna doing some chores: "Make her bed, pick up any debris around her bed, get dressed for the day, and do her hair, brush her teeth. And then she can go on her tablet." The children also attend an after-school program so they are not home until about 7 pm. Helen describes the time that the family re-unites:

> You would think my sanity would be while they're gone. But my sanity is when everybody's back home and (pause) I'm hearing Josh laughing in the next room and Sienna singing whatever it is on her tablet. Elisa listening to her whatever she's got going on her music—And being able to talk and laugh and joke with them. When they're all home and then when Dad comes home, 'cause that makes it complete 'cause he's usually the last to get home. When we all gather in the room just talking, communicating.

Helen and Ben continued to share the kinds of things they do together as a family, including special outings to Chuck E. Cheese, which Josh and Sienna love, and to the annual state fair. They celebrate holidays together. Josh loves to help out in the kitchen when Helen cooks. Josh can sometimes be protective of Sienna, but Ben, laughing, says: "They're close, but at the same time they can't stand each other." Elisa, being so much older, is like a second mother to them at times. However, they don't always listen to her when she tries to discipline them. Helen shares:

> They have their moments they pick to be loving to her and then they have their moments that they, you know, you're not the boss of me! You know, so I feel like it's more with their (pause) condition that they're brutally honest, you know. So if I don't like something you're doing, I'm gonna let you know.

Helen talked about her individual relationships with each of her children, stressing that she now sees Elisa more as an adult who she can share concerns with, while "with Sienna and Josh, it's more comical. We laugh a lot." Sienna often says silly things to make her laugh, and Josh can be very sweet:

> He'll come and hug me just out of the blue, especially if he feels like I'm being really very nice to him ... we went to the Night Out celebration the other night. In the middle of the program, I mean he's playing games, having a good time. In the middle of all of that, I'm sitting down, he comes and gives

me a hug and a kiss on my cheek … So I'm guessing he's saying, 'Thanks, Mom, for bringing us,' if he could say it, you know?

Ben shared his feelings about his relationships with the children:

> With Sienna, it's (pause) still a work in progress because I try to communicate with her for the most part, I love her and I know she knows she loves me. With Josh, it's like I just play around with him … And with Elisa, I just treat her like a grown-up, just like less, show less discipline with her now. And I'll give her advice when she needs it.

"I'm trying to teach them the main things."

When asked "What are some special things your children learn from being a part of your family?" both Ben and Helen talked about the ways they teach them by setting a good example. Helen articulated further:

> I feel like I'm trying to teach them, to love others, to love yourself, be respectful. (pause) … I'm learning to love myself, so I'll have Sienna say to herself every morning, 'I'm smart, kind, and important, and chubby girls are awesome!' … So that's how I'm getting Sienna, 'cause it's hard as a heavyset woman to love your body and love yourself and I don't want her to go through the self-esteem issues I went through as a young girl. And then probably Elisa went through. And you know, this is my second chance, you know?

And Ben added: "To be responsible adults. By me being an example, by me doing the right thing and hoping they pick up on it."

"Grow a thick skin. Be strong. Don't settle."

Asked about any advice from others that has been particularly helpful for their family, Helen recalled being told that as a mother of children with autism, she needed to grow a thick skin. She said she would definitely pass that advice on to others, to be strong and not to settle, "especially when it comes to your IEPs." (laughs) She added: "Make sure you've done your research. Take every opportunity to teach when you can." She shared an example:

> I have a sign in front of my house—"autistic child"—that people ask me about … I'm surprised in this day and age the people that don't know about autism. I tell them it's a neurological disorder. It's not retarded. It's not what people think of it to be. It's a neurological disorder and it means they process stuff differently.

Helen said it makes her feel powerful to have an answer for their questions.

"Make sure you have a passion for this because this is not just for a paycheck."

As the conversation came to a close, Helen and Ben offered some advice for professionals. From Helen, "Have patience, be kind and loving, and also have a thick skin" and from Ben, "Make sure you have a passion for this because this is not just for a paycheck." After the interview, Helen followed up with an email: "I just thought of something I wanted to add about Josh and naming him. When he was born we named him Joshua because that meant God's mouthpiece. I knew one day that he would speak volumes to many people."

Questions for Discussion

1. How would you describe the Foster family's strengths and resources?
2. How does this family work together to support their children and each other?
3. How would you characterize the Foster family's communication and collaboration with professionals?
4. This family shares examples of how difficult it can be to deal with insensitive responses to their children's challenging behavior in public. As a professional, how can you advocate for improved societal awareness and sensitivity towards people with disabilities?
5. Helen and Ben are dealing with the developmental emergence of puberty in both of their children. Reflect on the very different advice Helen received from extended family members and professionals in regard to Sienna. How can professionals help families protect their children's rights through life transitions?

5

A MOTHER RECLAIMS HER STRENGTH AND CONFIDENCE NEGOTIATING THE COMPLEXITIES OF SCHOOLING FOR HER CHILD

Maja and I first met when Viktor began attending the university-affiliated child care center where I worked as faculty director. Both parents, originally from Serbia, had been in the US for several years. Viktor was 2 years old and was receiving Early Intervention (EI) services but did not yet have a clear diagnosis. He had been given the label of Pervasive Developmental Disorder (PDD). He spent a year in our inclusive toddler classroom before moving to another site, a self-contained special education preschool. I continued to stay in touch with Viktor's family and they readily responded when asked to participate in the Conversations with Families Project. Due to their schedules, only Maja was available for the interview. We met in my office at the university and spoke for about two hours. At the time we met, Viktor was 8 years old.

Asked to describe her family, Maja shared:

> Yeah. My husband Stefan, he works here at [the University] (sighs) Viktor who is eight years old now … Yeah, that's my immediate family. Just the three of us. And an important part of the family … are occasionally with us. Physically, it's my Mom who is actually coming this Thursday. She comes from Serbia at least once a year for a few months. My Dad who never comes here, we have to go to see him, but Viktor's very attached to him. Stefan's Mom, who we don't see that much but … Viktor knows her and we know her and we have some relationship, but that's it.

She added: "… and I have a sister, yes, I have a sister who lives in France and because we're all spread out, we don't get to, I mean the last ten years, I've seen my sister twice."

"This hurt existed before I walked into their lives."

When I asked about her husband's family, Maja replied: "He has a brother. No relationship so I can't say anything." She shared that Viktor's father and his brother, who both live in the US now, had been estranged over something that happened a long time ago. She supports her husband's stance, saying:

> ... there is a line that I cannot cross ... And sometimes with something very hurtful, it was something so hurtful, I mean there's definitely love there, big love and care, but it's just something that's so hurtful that this is the only possible way to cope and deal with it.

Yet, it also is painful to her that Viktor is missing out by not having his uncle and cousins in his life. She shares:

> His brother has two daughters Viktor's age who are typically developing, but they will never have probably relationships since they're growing up already apart. So that's the part that personally affects me and, but like I said, this, this hurt existed before I walked into their lives, and Stefan's life in particular. I know one side of the story only. You know, I'm sure there is another side of the story, but of course, Stefan is my husband and he's a good husband to me and I have no doubts about him, but there is—I just see the big hurt ... I just see like the big shield of protection with this gesture, yeah. So that's it ... I think it's my husband's struggle that he needs to address on his own.

"I was afraid to face my family with it."

As we talked about her relationships with other extended family members, Maja said more about the significance of her mother in Viktor's life: "... my Mom is the biggest extension of us. She is almost like a part of our family because she really comes here a lot. She adores Viktor, Viktor's attached to her, we see each other a lot." She also mentioned her father and added that her cousins in Serbia are treated almost like siblings; "culturally, in the old days at least, it used to be that way."

She talked about how hard it was for her to take Viktor to Serbia "especially since we found out about the diagnosis ... mostly because I was afraid to face my family with it ..." She said at first, she and her husband thought: "this might be passing, this might be some phase, and I don't want to label him and people to label him for something that he might not even remember ... maybe it's some developmental hiccup." As time went on, she said, "I was going through the turbulence of emotions and acceptance ..." and finding that it

> was very difficult to accept that ... this is what it is ... And I was very fragile, I didn't have room for anyone else and anyone else's reaction—it was easier

for me to deal with people like therapists, teachers, people without emotional connection versus people who were a big part of my past and who expect certain things of my life the same way I did.

"I think this was the moment when I finally accepted it all."

As a way of finally letting her extended family know about Viktor's diagnosis, Maja enlisted her mother as the messenger. "… I ordered my Mom to keep telling everyone, not to hide it, not to try to downplay it, because she would do me a favor if people do not get shocked."

She talked about how difficult it was to take this step:

> … it's also combatting the cultural difference, people who are not autism savvy or disability savvy, people who never faced it before with the family members, refuse to educate themselves about them thinking that this is not going to be a part of their life forever. So it was a very big battle with my immediate family with whom I was in touch to kind of help me reach out to the [extended] family … and it wasn't even a question of hiding. It was just my inability to face anybody's reaction and questions and curiosity about it, like I want people to find out on their own and then deal with it.

During a short trip to Serbia not long before our interview, Maja was pleasantly surprised by her extended family's response to her and to Viktor. She shared an anecdote about getting together with her cousins and their children:

> … they came to see me during the day and we were outside. And of course, they saw Viktor up and down, left and right, everything and they loved him and they embraced him, even the kids. The girl was his age. She was like, you know, she picked it up like—as he was trying to run away, she was like protecting him and she asked when is he going to come back, you know? Such love and attention. First of all, Viktor enjoyed it, and second of all, it was such a revelation for me, and I think this was the moment when I finally accepted it all, like it doesn't matter. I don't mind. This is who he is, this is just fine. And I didn't even know that this was such a big burden on me.

She added:

> … he was really affectionate with all of them, he was smiling, he was giggling, and you know, he showed his worst part, he was running away, but they had so much fun with him, and … that brought me and Viktor closer …

As Maja and Viktor shared this joyful space with her extended family, she realized that the strong bonds she had with her cousins when she was growing up were still there.

And our relationship become closer after that. Like you know … I'm not really alone, this is not something that's strange and that I have to deal with alone, just with therapists, and … that bond with my family didn't shake because of this … [it] just meant a lot to me. Yeah.

And Viktor had such a good time that "… he was crying in the airplane … He didn't want to come back. Like you know, it is how I grew up."

"I completely lost my base and the core of how I was as a parent, who I was."

As Maja continued to reflect on the comfort of being accepted and loved unconditionally by her family, she began to share her early experiences parenting Viktor, before their lives were changed by Early Intervention.

I had all these developmental ideas in my head how I'm going to raise him … how I'm going to let him explore and find himself and build his self-esteem and his relationship with community, and I'm not going to help him out unless it's really necessary and unless I need to protect him … and this is how it was the first eighteen months and this is why we had such a beautiful relationship; then he was so confident. But … between eighteen and twenty months … when we were told by early intervention people … that he has PDD (Pervasive Developmental Disorder) … it was hard for us to accept because we didn't see any negative about him. We were so infatuated by Viktor, we didn't think about any delays, even though, yeah, yeah, right, he doesn't have five words, but you know, like (laughs) I mean he has so many other things …

Once he began to receive services, "all these facts enter in that world with professionals, with therapists, with various people with various backgrounds telling me all these different things, it was all negative, negative, negative, and … pointing to what he cannot do." She lamented that everything was done and said "in order to get the services … They're all doing their job in order to prove to somebody who will never see Viktor" that he needs particular services. She added, "and at the same time, they need to terrorize us. At least that's how our family got it, you know? We (pause) were those people who always pointed out what he can do."

Maja talked about her experiences at parent support meetings where she would hear negative things about every child.

For a while, I thought, oh my God, the poor children, they must be in really difficult shape. And then by the years, I got to meet the children … and I'm thinking, oh my God, it's just how parents perceive this situation and we perceived it so lovingly with Viktor that we thought that he was such an amazing person … We only pointed to [the] positive and it turns out that he is the kid with the most issues of everybody else we met.

She continued,

> … we got sucked into that world, we got sucked into that negativity about he doesn't know, do this, he should be doing that, he should be doing this. We had a very stressful few years with him and we were really probably bad parents. I mean, making so many mistakes, trying to push him, trying to make him behaving appropriately, being so important that he's socially (pause) you know, and I completely lost my base and the core of how I was as a parent, who I was. I'd become some strict (pause) lady, but then again, I still have so much emotion, I was probably wishy-washy. I don't even know, you know, like how it was, but I already became some disciplinarian because I thought, okay, this is the kid who needs that.

Now, however, she feels happy that she is "… coming back to how I was … For six years it was a struggle, but now we're coming back with the same emotions." She seemed almost triumphant as she said, "You know what? I don't care what the world thinks. He is what he is. I don't care if he screams in public, people need to accept him as long as he's not endangering someone … stealing, you know." She went on to say

> I have to be myself, he has to be himself … I need to support him as a parent and love him and hug him as many times as he needs and tell him everything nicely. I don't have to raise my voice. Even if he doesn't want to do something for the first time, you know, like who cares? … Instead of changing him, I feel like I really need to advocate for him and his community because they are different. They're smart, they're aware, they've very sensitive emotionally. But just they're different … and they cannot unfortunately (pause) in a classical, in a classic way, they cannot defend themselves.

"Both of us are loving parents to him and … we do many things together."

As our conversation continued, Maja and I approached another guiding question together.

INTERVIEWER: … another one of my questions is, what do you see as the major strengths of your family? And I think you've been talking about that.

MAJA: Yeah.

INTERVIEWER: Talking about what made you, I don't know how you would describe it, but you know, what I'm hearing you say is that you have something really powerful to give him as a mother and you're letting yourself do that.

MAJA: Yes. You probably described it better than I would. (laughs)

Maja went on to share that they did have a strong family bond, saying, "… both of us are loving parents to him and we do many things together. We've never excluded him because he has special needs."

Maja talked more about how she and Stefan travel with Luka, including him in their activities in a very natural way. She said,

> He travels with us, he goes on airplanes, we vacation with him, we take him on excursion day trips. He has lots of experience. Probably it's great for him. We didn't even question it, but it was just—of course, he's a part of our family …

They are willing to make accommodations if needed that allow the family to have the best experiences when they travel, such as renting an apartment with an extra room for Viktor to insure a better night's sleep. Maja added: "… we as a family have this lifestyle that, you know, the three of us as kind of a team, and I think that's, that is a strength of our family. Yes."

"It sounds so easy now but you know, it took me so much time to get here."

As our conversation turned to those things that are going especially well for Viktor and the family, Maja reiterated how happy she is to be enjoying her life with him again.

> … I'm so glad in my mind and in my soul and in my heart [that] I came back to how I was with him when we had the great relationship before we got to the tornado of the diagnosis and I was lost … I felt like I was trained to be an unnatural parent to him …

She talked about how guilty she felt when Viktor first received his diagnosis, and how she asked herself what she did wrong as a parent. Was he not talking because he was at home with her and not in a child care setting? She shared, "It sounds now silly but that's what you're so sure of at the beginning … that you are not doing a good job …"

She talked more about how happy she was to be a mother to Viktor before the diagnosis and how wonderful it felt to have those feelings once again.

> And now I feel the same way in a similar way. I don't feel him—like there was a part, all this six years when I've felt … him as a burden, somebody I

need rest from, somebody [who] ... was burdening me down ... But I've changed (pause) with something internally changing in me about ... our relationship and I enjoy again being with him. I don't mind spending the day with him, taking him along with me, even if I need to run errands, you know? ... I notice I'm comfortable now being with him ... in any environment.

Maja provided several anecdotes to describe how she was now taking a more proactive stance in dealing with situations that arise, particularly in the outside world. In one example, she took Viktor with her to a doctor's appointment, where he got restless;

the doctor was shocked ... but I'm like, "Listen, I just need a refill and, you know, we had to go. This is who he is, you know?" And in a way, I was glad that somebody saw, like the people, more people I'm dealing with know him, see him versus know about him.

In another example, she talked about having to wait in line to pick up a number for a race she was running in.

It was so crowded of course to pick a number and wow, and everything that would go against him. So I went to pick up the number, I was explaining to him all the time what's going on, that we have to be this and that. Whatever gadgets I could find I gave him so he's like looking at them. And finally, when I bought something, I asked the guy, "Can you please, how can I cut the line? I mean, I understand if I cannot, I'll try, but he, he has autism, he might burst out, he might not, but if you can do something about it, help me out." And he did. So you know, I'm getting more comfortable with this.

In further explaining how different she is feeling about Viktor's behavior, she said,

I was always waiting, Viktor, wait like everybody else, and I was always justifying in my head, wow, he needs to learn, you know? Now I'm like, Listen, he doesn't need to learn. And if he said no, we're going to try ... and I would not now [take it] to heart if somebody says no. For all these years, if somebody said anything insensitive towards his diagnosis, I would have a tantrum, (laughs) you know?

She added:

So you know, I set the tone. Everybody understands. And people are helpful then. This is something that's working for me now. I think this is where I grew. And it took me so much time. It sounds so easy now but you know, it took me so much time to get here. It took me so much time.

"I just would like for people to feel comfortable around him."

Asked "what would you like other people to understand about Viktor?" Maja's response was simple and so deeply felt. She talked about the ways that Viktor and others with social and learning differences are too often excluded, shunned, or even feared due to a lack of knowledge about their disability.

> I just would like for people to feel comfortable around him. I want people to be more aware, to know more basic stuff about how people with autism present themselves and they're not scary people ... like, some people would remove themselves if they're near to us or wait for another elevator ... That can be hurtful ...

She talked about other people's lack of awareness and acceptance, reflecting back on the ways that the toddlers in our inclusive classroom tried to learn about Viktor by asking so many questions and wanting to understand him. She said, "... many times I was caught off-guard, even as his Mom ... But I would like all that to be more familiar. I would like parents not to have stigma because kids are fine."

Maja shared more about the experiences she and Viktor have had at community playgrounds where children are often attracted to Viktor but "the parents are like distracting them with the facial expressions saying, 'Don't follow that kid,' you know?" She said, "that I would love to change because they're wrong. Viktor has so much to offer. He's a great kid. He has so many strengths. And I see why kids are attracted to him." She talked about how children are often curious about him and the ways he plays, "I mean, first of all, he's a cute boy" and he is also physically very competent "... he's proactive, he knows how to run, he knows how to climb." She would love for this to change: "... it would be better for them, for other kids to know that there are kids who have certain limitations because they [also] have limitations, I'm sure, in some other areas."

"All what I want other people to be."

When asked what she had learned about herself through Viktor, Maja paused – "Oh my God. That's a very complex question." She talked about her own strength saying:

> ... actually, I thought about myself as a strong person before I even got into this situation, but (sighs) (long pause) I definitely expanded my horizons with Viktor. I've become more accepting, more compassionate, more aware, all what I want other people to be! (laughs)

Maja said she sees herself as "More loving and ... in a positive way able to ... understand and love and be compassionate towards people that I wasn't, wouldn't maybe be if Viktor wasn't ... the kid that he is and I wasn't his Mom." She commented further: "Like I'm not only talking about people, kids with disabilities, but with any kind of struggles, addictions. I think I have definitely changed my inner feelings about that."

Reflecting back on her own early life, Maja shared:

> I had an uncle who was always—he didn't have any diagnosis but he was bad at school and he had like childish behavior even as an adult and always wanted to be, kind of very playful, which was cute and funny but some-times ... we were always rolling our eyes at him, "well, how could he do something so stupid? This was so irresponsible of him" ... but you know, I've just come to realize now that it's not his fault ... That's how he is, and I try to advocate for him to my Mom ... so that's what changed in me. I probably wouldn't think about my uncle. I would just be like, Oh yeah, he's very immature ... but this has changed, and ... I mean I'm glad (pause) ... that I feel the way I feel ... it's an important growth, you know, spiritual if you would say, emotional. My emotional capacity is even richer now and stronger ... acceptance and understanding wider of people's weaknesses, less judgmental.

"If we start scolding him now all the time, all the time, he will lose interest."

As our conversation moved to talking about goals and dreams for Viktor, Maja did not hesitate to say:

> For him to be independent. That's always been the dream, goal, and fear at the same time. I am at the same time terrified what he's going to do without me ... I really would like him to be independent, and to be aware of the danger, to be able to protect himself.

She also had a lot to say about the role of educators and other professionals in helping achieve those goals.

One of the things that Maja feels gets in the way of educating children like Viktor is an over-emphasis on discipline at the expense of moving learning forward.

> The problem that I see occurring ... in [the] education system so far is that ... the big emphasis, to me too big, is on discipline and on behavioral problems. To me it's unnecessary because some kids will never change. These kids will never maybe sit in a chair. They may always be wiggling around the room and eating, you know, and it doesn't matter. This is not a life-changing situation, but some educators won't move into the next step, educational problems, unless they teach them the basic behavior, which

could take forever, and then all else is neglected. So I disagree with that, but that's what is around everywhere and if the kid is not behaving in the school, he's going to be expelled. As a matter of fact, Viktor was expelled.

She went on to talk about how important she thinks it is for educators to be able to "see through their behavior. Nobody saw through Viktor's behavior ..." She shared an example from one of the first times she brought Viktor to a toddler playgroup when he was not yet 18 months old.

He was the only kid in the classroom ... who could do the puzzle. This was not a simple puzzle for that age ... but he wouldn't sit in a circle. He would sit two seconds and he would go and run around, and he was always scolded, always, always scolded, and nobody ever noticed about the puzzle. Nobody once praised him and said about it, and to me, [that] he was capable to figure out what to do without any instructions with the puzzle was a big deal. I was so proud of him but I was the only one, I was alone.

This example from early in Viktor's life still stands out for Maja as it depicts what continues to be a struggle for him educationally. Maja described how at that time she felt very fragile and was not able to advocate for Viktor. She shared,

... they think you're weird, you're odd, and Viktor doesn't present what they need and want, and all they wanted from him is to sit in a circle during the story time. And I was forcing him to sit in a circle.

She added:

So that's what I would like to change. I would like teachers from the beginning to see through that behavior, especially if it's not aggressive, it's not harming anyone. And not only to ignore it as a negative behavior, but to see, to focus on what kids can do, and to see that, oh, this kid might run forever and he probably will be a wiggly and restless child forever. Let me just make sure he doesn't lose the interest for his mind because if we start scolding him now all the time, all the time, he will lose interest, which happened to Viktor, by the way. It did. You know, when you always [hear] 'This is wrong, This is wrong, Don't do this, Don't do that,' like of course he doesn't want to do it.

Another related area of importance for Maja is for educators and other professionals "... not to underestimate kids like Viktor, which they do all the time even now." She offered a few metaphors, such as practicing swimming, and having the teacher constantly point out that you are not turning your arm in just the right way, even though you can already swim; or attending a yoga class where the teacher talks too much so that you are "… not listening and … annoyed and … exhausted after that yoga." She said:

> … this is what happens to Viktor. And I have inner feeling sometimes I identify with him in certain classes when I get bored … So it all depends on the approach, if you want to over-explain to these kids which I think Viktor has been, and I think he is still in the school setting where he's now … I would like those kids to be more challenged intellectually and educationally.

"We don't want him to be sad, we don't want him to feel ever like there's nothing …"

In addition to these ways of working with children, Maja also offered other ideas for schools to take up regarding support for more inclusion and understanding on the part of parents. She suggested that schools could provide better ways of communicating with parents about the significance of including all children. She said she had not seen that here but she could remember this happening in her home country, "… but you know, here, don't interfere in the private lives …" She added:

> … you don't need to interfere, nobody needs to interfere in a private life, but just to emphasize … how it is important and everybody is invited to the birthday party … what does it mean developmentally? … to pay attention to … group belonging in the developmental stages, not just leave it to one, [but] to be everybody's personal business.

In illustrating this point further, Maja talked about how as a runner, she herself has benefited so much from being part of a team.

> Like nobody is left behind, we all carry each other, like you know, no matter how slow, how fast, we were cheering each other. That was a great feeling and a big part of my achievement, a big part why I made it through.

She shared that as one of the slower runners, she really benefited from having that group support, and she sees that sense of community really lacking for children like Viktor.

> I mean, we don't know each other, we don't know who does what in their private lives, but running is our thing and we support each other. And even if we go out, outside of running, we are cheering and supporting each other in life, but like it's a community, and so that's what I think is missing, especially for these kids who are not, who don't know how to appropriately approach their peers. Viktor is not anti-social. He doesn't know how to play. That's a difference.

Maja spoke more on this topic, describing Viktor as a child who "loves people." Yet, she continued,

> We never got invited anywhere pretty much. I mean, for that, thank God we are his parents. That's probably why we all travel and all this excitement that we bring extra that his life even looks more fabulous that's to make up for that ... We don't want him to be sad, we don't want him to feel ever like there's nothing, but it would be great for him if he had the kids that he sees on a regular basis and he had like, like five unsuccessful play dates and then sixth one is going to be great, you know? ... that would be great.

In her mind's eye, Maja sees the school as the responsible place to educate other parents about building a community for all of the children. She also added that it was important for the information coming to parents to draw on research, because "parents like to hear something that's not just somebody's opinion." In thinking about the value of providing this kind of enrichment for parents, she reflected back on herself:

> Look how I describe myself and my growth because before Viktor, I was always a loving and tolerant person, but I only could understand things that I could identify with, that was part of my experience. Now what's changed for me, I'm able to be empathetic for many things that never were part of my personal experience, and that's what is growth, that's enrichment actually.

"I was very traumatized by the school system"

As we began to discuss Viktor's educational experiences in more depth, Maja recalled that when he started at our university-affiliated child care center he was already receiving services through Early Intervention. At age 3, the family was encouraged to move Viktor from our inclusive setting into a segregated special education program. They were given a couple of options for preschools and chose the one closest to their home. Viktor attended this school for two years. Maja described this experience in the following way:

> ... he was tolerating well, being there ... but Stefan and I never had the feeling that [the school] offered him any opportunity to grow and express himself. To the contrary, I think he was repressed ... Viktor was always [the] only non-verbal kid and he was always just following to the activities without any attention to him in a way how can he complete the task independently ... or like people would do things for him or just make him don't do anything. And if he would cry and be frustrated, they would walk him out, they would take him and walk him outside and again, without any understanding why did he come out ...

When she and her husband talked with the school about what they felt was a lack of attention to Viktor's learning needs, they brought in a paraprofessional to work one on one with him. However, Maja did not think this was the best solution to the problem because "it's not that he needs that much one on one but just more opportunity to express himself." Although they did not believe the setting was the best for Viktor, she said, "… because we just didn't know what else to do, so we stayed in the situation hoping that something's going to happen on its own." When Viktor was ready to transition to kindergarten, they were happy to find a place for him in a new experimental program at another specialized school where he would be one of four children in a class with three professionals working collaboratively.

At first, things seemed to be going well at the new school. "Viktor was there for almost two years." But something happened near the end of his time there that came as a total shock to Maja and her husband.

> We loved the school, we loved the devotion to the students, we loved the sense of community that they built with us parents and with the students. They did pretty close to what I was describing I would want. But if the time comes that they think that your child is not a good fit for them … they expel you mercilessly.

Maja described how Viktor was unexpectedly "expelled in the middle of the school year" when she thought everything was going well.

> I was called by the director with whom I had a great relationship … I was fundraising for the school … She said we have bad news. And then all of a sudden, all this negativity about him. He is misbehaving, he is this, he is laying down on the floor, nobody can pick him up. And … he was always like that. Nothing that they told me was new so I just didn't see how he was great, great, great, [and] all of a sudden … something was really … mismanaged very much … but what was very hurtful, it affected so negatively me and Viktor, and me, I know for me, (pause) I don't know what condition I had, but it put me to bed that I couldn't get up for two weeks.

Maja went on to describe the onslaught of feelings she was overwhelmed by: "I felt betrayal, shock, loss, grief, out of strength, what do I do now? Like I didn't see this coming, you know?" She described how the school gave her an explanation – "they were very good with words. But I don't, honestly, believe those words." She saw that they were using "legally correct terms" to make sure they were covering their bases. For her that "was a big disappointment and trauma, trauma. How do I trust anyone with my child anymore?" Because this happened in the middle of the school year, she "negotiated with them to keep him part-time, which was basically (pause) what happened, until the end of the year so he can graduate." However, those last months at the school were very difficult for Maja and Viktor:

> that was very painful because he was already outcast … all the teachers and therapists who embraced me in the hallways were like shying away from me … (pause) and I still was the same person, I was even accepting that I was leaving … I would always say hi to everyone I had relationships [with]. My feelings were always if I thought you were a good school and good teacher today, I'm going to think about that next day, no matter what you do to me, you know? … [that] really made me question sincerity of the whole thing and the future. And so I was very traumatized by the school system. One school was bad, the second school was better but end up being worse with the experience, so I really wanted to just lock down and not go to school to protect (pause) That was my gut feeling. Survival.

As she began to search for another school for Viktor, she found herself carrying over the effects of this traumatic experience. She "didn't want to push" to get Viktor into a school "because I never wanted to end up where I was with this school. If somebody really doesn't want him the way he is, no, no."

Maja and Stefan searched tirelessly for the best program for Viktor. They even considered one program that was outside of the city, but Maja shared, "it was too much for me. I didn't even look into that because I knew I didn't have it in me to get engaged that way." She said, "we called everybody we knew to ask about what should we do in such circumstances … the therapists didn't want to work with him." She talked about how one very well-known psychotherapist who focuses on autism said, "I don't want to work with him because he is too special needs for me and—I'm too old for him." Although this came as a disappointment to them, Maja and Stefan found her advice helpful and appreciated her "holistic approach."

Maja added:

> Like most psychotherapists don't treat autism, they just give medication, and she was that one, the only one we found … but she didn't want to work with us, with Viktor specifically (pause) and she wasn't kind with her words also. She said like, Oh, this kid is so strange, I've never seen a kid like him. Either he is like something's really wrong with him or you did, or all you did so far with him in terms of therapy was wrong.

Maja even talked to her own therapist about the psychotherapist's response to them regarding Viktor and was surprised as he explained "Well, she's an old school. (laughs) You know, that's how the old school therapists used to be … they can say whatever they want …"

Maja summed things up this way:

So nobody wants to work with him, school expelled him, so our lawyer at the time … gave us the name of this therapeutic program … and we called and emailed them a few times. They had a website, it looked good. It's based on Applied Behavior Analysis (ABA) but you know what? We've never been in ABA before, maybe we need to go to the ABA … maybe we fought it for … too long for the wrong reason. Maybe that's where we belong.

The cost of this private program was prohibitive for the family, "… (sighs) they're financially (pause) they're so expensive, it's like impossible for many, many families." But they were able to secure a personal loan from a friend to help them pay the fees. Although Maja felt that "the therapists in the program knew what they were doing in one on one" she found that it was very different from what Viktor was used to; "… it was not that organized. It wasn't the school setting, it wasn't the structured day that happens, that Viktor knew what to expect." She said it "felt more like a special needs day care" and even though the therapists were able to respond effectively to his behavior, "he was losing his routine … so then I knew we had to just look for the school setting after all …"

Maja began to think about homeschooling Viktor, having teachers come in to work with him, but realized she didn't have the resources to do this.

> I don't have capacity to homeschool him by myself. I don't have financial means to afford the teachers. I would homeschool him only if I was able to afford teachers to come to structure his day and to pay the teachers. I would actually love to do that. Actually, I still think it might be good for him, because in that case I can control the curriculum and academics, which they underestimate him.

Meanwhile, they are suing the Department of Education (DOE) for funding for Viktor's program. The DOE had not paid for his education for the past two years because they are questioning why he went to a specialized therapeutic program rather than to a school. At the time of our meeting, Viktor was attending another new program which seemed to be going fine in some ways:

> After what I've been through, I can say I'm happy there because I've been through hell and back. If I haven't been through hell and back, who knows, you know? But considering how … my situation was really (pause) turbulent, and stressful, and traumatic, like at least again, our life is structured, he goes there, he gets one on one, they like him, they embrace him, they don't shy away from behaviors that come with autism.

However, she still had concerns about his educational needs not being met:

> But they work with him like he was a one and-a-half year old, that is the big problem. So I got to realize that you have to do this at home … and you

know ... most children with special needs, no matter what school they go and no matter on what end of the spectrum are they, all of them have tutors at home and ... none of [the parents] are happy with the academics approach and expectations for their children.

She reflected on a discussion she had with other parents of children with special needs about this:

And we are thinking like, we were even laughing at the time. Like look at us, we're paying so much for these schools and then we have to think what we're going to do after because, not because we are so ambitious, we want our kids to go to Harvard, but just to get the basic out of it.

Maja had some final thoughts to add about educational experiences for children like Viktor:

First of all, I would ban to expel, to be allowed to expel any kids with special needs from school, like for even neuro-typical kids, you know what it means for their self-esteem, for their development, for everything, expelling the child, I think it's a crime ... And all these schools ... they look great on paper ... you almost want to cry when you read about them. We accept these children ... with all the differences, and you know ... —it's not true, it's such a lie.

She added:

I think the state is spending so much money on these kids, but I don't think it's in the right way. I don't think it's in the right way. And you know what also is an important thing, especially I would like this to go on the record. I think it's very unfair that all these kids get the same diagnosis. Autism covers so many different children. And they are so different. They have to kind of (pause) stop diagnosing ... because it's not fair for my son to be on paper the same as a kid who's going to an integrated program in public school when my son cannot go, cannot ever be accepted. You know, and on the paper for somebody who is deciding their future in DOE, they look exactly the same because everybody is going to write all the negative things ... to get the diagnosis.

"Our diagnosis is very costly in school-wise and everything else."

From the start there seemed to be some confusion about Viktor's diagnosis of PDD. Maja talked about how the first doctor they saw:

... underlined a more verbal apraxia and dyspraxia, not autism ... she even told us, which is not politically correct for her to assume, but we liked to hear it, she even thought that if he resolved his speech that he may lose his autism and stay with ADHD.

Later, when Viktor was being evaluated for a kindergarten placement, he was given the label of autism. However, Maja expressed concern about making a quick diagnosis for Viktor who doesn't easily fit a clear profile. Maja had this to say about psychiatrists who work with children with disabilities:

> … they usually just wanna just give you a prescription after two seconds seeing your child. And I'm open towards medication right now if that can help him contain and manage, but not in a way that somebody can see him for two seconds. No, no.

Maja continued to share her concerns about the ways that medication is being used for very young children as a tool for navigating the school system.

> You know, many parents have children who are capable of being in the main-stream classrooms, but they are wiggly and parents want to resolve that with the medication. And … there are some parents whose kids go to schools that do not accept IEP kids so they need to hide the diagnosis, so they will medicate to hide the diagnosis. We are not one of those parents. I want Viktor to feel better and to help him calm him down in a way that he can learn, that he can move ahead, and you know, not pleasing the environment in terms of the school …

She also expressed concern about how easily these medications are being dispensed.

> and you know, I'm also very disappointed, the doctors are very (pause) easy to give you very serious medications, psychotic medications. Like very, very serious for somebody so young for not knowing the child … it's scary and I don't trust those doctors.

She reiterated what she believes is needed from doctors who are positioned to prescribe these drugs

> in my book, I would have either a high level of psychotherapist or a medical doctor who would really have this holistic approach, who will get to know the child, see him regularly for six months, and then decide, I think this medication will be good for him. I think that [they] should take more ser-iously giving it to children … but I'm alone in this, very, very alone.

With regard to Viktor, Maja shared that she has recently found a new doctor who does take a more holistic approach: "so far, she is somebody I may trust, I'm still not sure. But like I'm curious to see her again." At the same time that she is impressed by the thoroughness with which this new doctor is approaching Viktor's care, she also seemed a little suspicious about some of the doctor's ideas. For example, Maja doesn't "believe in these diets ... what color is this food and that food." Unfortunately, "insurance doesn't cover her and a visit is four hundred dollars ... which you're going to pay even if you don't show up because you have a credit card on file."

Maja and Stefan continue their dedication to finding and doing what they believe is best for Viktor, despite the fact that his "diagnosis is very costly in school-wise and everything else. None of the professionals are covered ... They're all in thousands of dollars." However, "when it's your child, and people are recommending them, of course, you're going to come up with the way to do it." Maja also shared that she believes that "maybe if the people who are working with [children] with more challenges were paid more, maybe things would change ..."

She added:

> Like not to have same salary for somebody who works with kids who are just stuttering and kids who are nonverbal, it's not the same amount of work. So I understand that professionals are going to resist, resent kids like Viktor because they have to sweat and still be an unknown what this kid wants to say ... if they have different diagnoses ... and then this kind of professional works with Viktor ... with a salary like the doctors ... because somebody who is not personally involved has to be motivated to work with these children. And I think the lack of motivation to work with kids like Viktor leave them behind.

"We were there to put him in this situation, in spite of our fears."

When asked about a special activity that Viktor enjoys with his family, Maja responded without hesitation: "Skiing!" She added: "And he's able to do it ... and this year was the first year that I was able to do it with him alone." She shared a story about how she and Viktor "were stuck on the top of the mountain —they kicked us out from some restaurant and Stefan wasn't there so I had to go down with Viktor, and I was so proud of both of us." Although usually Viktor skis with his dad, this time Maja had to be the one to guide him. She said:

> I'm not an avid skier. I'm okay. I would never take responsibility ... for someone. And Viktor knew how to ski with Stefan but he doesn't listen [to] directions. So ... like Momma Bear—I was always making sure I'm in front of him. All of a sudden, my skiing skills improved. (laughs)

She described how she skied in front of Viktor: "I was zigzagging, and every time I was screaming 'Turn!' I think I was like a coach through the entire mountain. Everybody was listening to me. Turn, turn! And he was following me."

Reflecting on this experience, Maja said:

> And you know, I think these are the things, (pause) your relationship as a family, you know, brings you together. And this is the best thing that we have … that came from our family. If we were relying only on advices of people we worked with, Viktor would never step on the ski. He's very (pause) limited in every school how he is, his movement. Like I said, [it is] very underestimated what he can do. It was crazy but brave for my husband to put him on skis a few years ago and be persistent, and look at him now. He's skiing on a Black Diamond. And he's a good skier.

She added:

> So it's very important for kids' parents to try different things with their kids, no matter what … And yeah, that's —that's something that we did with him, that we were there to put him in this situation, in spite of our fears … Yes. I mean, of course, as parents, we're always going to be scared. We can never control them. But this is something that, you know, like we're going to see where we're going to go from there and we always have to build something up to be new.

"There's a story that went around about Italy and Holland."

Interestingly, when asked, "Is there a piece of advice that anybody gave you that was helpful to you?" Maja had trouble coming up with an easy response. After a long pause, she said:

> I feel like I'm sounding arrogant if I said no, so nothing comes to my head that's memorable, but this wasn't advice but there was something that hit me that I could identify with, never thought about. There's a story that went around about Italy and Holland, I don't know if you read it.

INTERVIEWER: Oh yes, I've seen that. Yes.

MAJA: I mean, that definitely made me cry but it could be helpful in looking at things in that perspective. It's like it's a wonder, it's not a destination you wanted to reach …

INTERVIEWER: You have to imagine something different …

MAJA: It's not the experience you planned for and you're gonna do this, you're going to go to this museum, you're going to see that, and you're going to eat pasta, and you know, like everything, and you go somewhere and you're like, 'Where am I?' This is cold and different and it's not the same climate and everything, and I didn't want to reach here, but then you discover Rembrandt. This is like actually the part when I was sold, you know? Like and other stuff like windmills and flowers uh, you know, and that's exactly something that, that's how it is in my case.

Maja said she knows "That story rubs different people in different ways." She added:

I wouldn't like to judge parents that much. I am following everything on Facebook that's autism related, including two groups that are created by autistic people, and ... they are very harsh on everybody in society, very, very harsh, uncomfortable ... if I wasn't curious for my own education, I would unfriend them. I'm always disturbed. But they're like, blame is put on parents for even having expectations. I mean, in an ideal world, we will not, nobody would have, but it's not realistic. We all expect what's known to us, how we see, you know, so I wouldn't blame parents and I would never, I would advise them never to feel guilty for feeling those negative [feelings], because that's normal. You know what's around you and you expect. You don't know how Holland can be if you haven't heard of it and planned for it and never seen it in your surrounding and your family, and it's challenging. So, it's okay for parents to feel the way they feel

"Somebody really needs to know the child."

Maja offered a few final thoughts as our conversation came to a close. She expressed how important she thought it was for those working with and parenting children with disabilities to "enlighten themselves on the topic, educate themselves from various sources." She said:

I've never seen any kid like Viktor and probably every parent can say that for their kid, but I definitely, I've been around kids with the same diagnosis on paper for six years and ... I've never seen anyone I can remotely compare to Viktor. And everybody thinks their child is very special, which it is, so I think that's why it's important to not go by what society expects or by what certain professionals say, but to really try to (pause) educate them ...

She shared that she has been to professional conferences in addition to reading and accessing other resources to learn more about Viktor's needs and different ways of responding to him. She has found that "it's very helpful to have so many different pieces and you're always going to find what matters to you." She talked about how challenging it is for teachers to work with children who have different learning styles and encouraged them to take a more eclectic approach. She also reiterated the significance of ensuring continuity by increasing teachers' salaries to reduce turnover.

> I would also say the same thing [to teachers]: do not follow the textbook with every kid. Do not tell parents what to do by the textbook … pick one student and focus on them. I think professionals should be dedicated to one student for at least one academic year and be motivated by a fair compensation for that … it doesn't matter what the classroom setting. It's more that somebody like really knows one kid, that's the only way …

Maja ended our conversation with one final hope: "So that is my final thought in advance for the better future, for our hope. I think it's the only way—somebody really needs to know the child."

Questions for Discussion

1. How would you describe Maja's and Stefan's family strengths and resources?
2. How do Maja and Stefan work together to support their child and each other?
3. How would you characterize Maja's communication and collaboration with professionals?
4. Maja speaks poignantly about how Viktor's diagnosis and her experiences with EI professionals "trained (her) to be an unnatural parent to him." How can professionals keep from compromising families' confidence in their own parenting and build on their intuitive strengths and unique understandings of their children?
5. In this story, we are given access to this parent's pain and frustration regarding professionals' inability to "see through" Viktor's challenging behavior. This is particularly powerful when she describes how traumatizing it was for her when Viktor was expelled from school. What issues does this raise regarding professionals' ethical responsibility to protect children's right to an appropriate education?

6

PARENTS COLLABORATE TO SUPPORT THEIR SONS' HEALTH AND EDUCATIONAL ACHIEVEMENT

The B family is accustomed to welcoming professionals and friends, and the many folks that blur those roles, into their home. The afternoon I stepped into was filled with lots of good energy and happy noise. Jen and Neil skillfully pivoted and tag-teamed between our conversation and time with their boys, Mitchell and Miller, and Mitchell's nurse, Diane, in the next room. It was clear that this was a well-practiced dance between them. I quickly decided to worry less about all the choreographed steps of my interview protocol and instead just try to follow their rhythm. For this reason, while some topics are addressed by both Jen and Neil, others are just responded to by one of them.

I first met Jen a few years ago when I interviewed her for a study designed to follow up with the children and families that had attended a university-based inclusive early childhood program I was affiliated with. She shared her family's story so thoughtfully and with such warm candor that I invited her to be a guest speaker in a class I teach on building partnerships with families of children with disabilities. Jen addressed my class for two semesters, and for her third visit, she brought along Neil, Mitchell, and Miller. These four "teachers" generously shared their lives and experiences with my students and me.

Jen took me on a tour of their home. She pointed out the track system with a motorized lift and sling that they use to lift Mitchell out of his bed and move him to the bathroom. She described it as an accommodation that helps them to care for Mitchell and allows him to be the most functional. She explained that her state has a fund to help pay for house modifications like the track system.

Their home was accented by photos and their boys' artwork. Jen showed me a painting that Mitchell made when he was 7. On the back of the frame was a photo of Mitchell in the process of painting it. She explained, "You can tell he is excited when they put the canvas in front of him. He chose his pictures, his colors, he did this with his hands, he used his sponges also ... for him that was one of the first times that he actually participated and got to do it himself." Jen also pointed out a collage that hung in Mitchell's bedroom that was created by one of his aides as a special end-of-the-year present. She explained:

> Each week the teacher would send home like a slip of paper that would say "What did you do this weekend?" ... And we started including pictures because Mitchell enjoyed looking at them and it was much more meaningful for him ... So his aide kept them all and cut the pictures out and scanned them ... and then the other half are things they did at school ... it was a special present, because she knew Mitchell and she knew that would be meaningful for him. So, when he's sitting in his room, he can look over and remember those times, you know?

"and now I'm on a colony."

At the time of the interview, Mitchell was 15 and Miller was 11. When asked to name the members of her family, Jen included her husband, Mitchell and Miller, and Casie, the family dog. She then widened the circle to include her mom and sister and Neil's family. She explained that, while they live far away, they communicate by phone and host them for visits a couple of times a year. She shared that her parents do their best to participate in events at the boys' schools passing on to their grandchildren the same value of education that they instilled in her. Jen went on to identify other important people in her family's life, starting with Mitchell's nurse, Diane, and explaining that all the nurses they've had over the years have added something important to their family, "when someone is in your home with you, their life gets melded with your own." She shared stories of nurses bringing their own children and special cultural dishes at Christmas and the B family attending their family events. She explained, "That's not true with every single person. Nurses are supposed to keep some professional distance ... you don't want to intrude, but you don't want to exclude either." Jen described other special connections with school bus drivers, and a former classroom aide who, many years later, is still a family friend.

Jen shared an anecdote about recently visiting Miller's previous early childhood program so that he could read a story to the children. Afterwards, Miller commented to his former teacher, "You know, my days at The Children's Center was like Mother England and now I'm on a colony" he went on to explain that he had brought what he needed from his time there with him. Perhaps that's a perfect metaphor for the way the B family carries with them what they've learned from professionals who have, in some way, for some time, "melded" their lives with theirs. I feel certain that this is a reciprocal process and there are many professionals on colonies who carry with them the lessons they've learned from Miller, Mitchell, and the whole B family.

"What is the most commonsense thing we can do here?"

Jen also shared that sometimes these connections don't happen the way you'd like; she described an experience at one of Mitchell's previous schools:

> I was trying to reach out and make connections with his teachers and the other people at school, and I was not able to do it. I could feel like resistance to it … it made me frustrated and very unhappy.

Both Mitchell and Miller received Early Intervention services. Mitchell's services were completely home-based and Jen characterized them as "glorious." Miller also began home-based Early Intervention services when he was approximately 18 months old and, like Mitchell, he received occupational therapy (OT), physical therapy (PT), and speech and language therapy (SLT). About nine months later, Miller started in an inclusive university-based early childhood program that he attended through preschool while receiving some additional private occupational therapy. Over the next several years, Jen and Neil worked together to navigate a range of schools, settings, and services for Mitchell and Miller.

Mitchell attended a self-contained preschool that, as Jen described, "never really worked out the way I had hoped. It wasn't bad, it just wasn't great." He transitioned to a different school for first grade but left in the middle of the schoolyear because Jen and Neil felt there were "safety issues, which were very upsetting." Everyone seemed to feel more comfortable with the next school that Mitchell attended. Jen felt "the people there really were oriented to solve problems and to make things happen more than any other place I've ever seen." Jen shared that Mitchell, who has cerebral palsy, experiences challenges in regard to self-regulation and sensory overload. She explained, "When someone's in a chair and is kind of strapped in, it's much easier to get overwhelmed because things are coming at you, you cannot move away from things, you cannot necessarily tell someone I need a break."

Mitchell communicates using a Tobii portable speech generating device that employs an eye gaze system. A camera picks up light reflections from his pupils and translates the movement of his eyes into cursor movements that convert text and symbols into a voice output. Jen described how Mitchell also uses his face and body to express when he's feeling a bit overwhelmed:

> You can see it on his face … he looks stressed, his body will get stiff. But he also can use his device to say I need to go, I need to go outside. He'll tell you what he needs. Sometimes for him, his body can become so stiff and have enough difficulty that he can't use his communication device anymore because it requires his body to be calm, like for him to be able to look and to select things on his device requires a somewhat calm body. So, there's a point at which he can't do that anymore. But when he can't say it with his device, I can oftentimes tell.

Jen continued to explain that, at his current school, Mitchell has developed a great number of skills and is expanding his overall self-mastery. But, most importantly, Mitchell has "really started to enjoy school!" Jen added, "it's a great environment for him, but it's not inclusive, you know, so that's the next hurdle."

Miller had started at the university-based Children's Center as a toddler with an Individualized Family Service Plan (IFSP). While there, he received in-class support as well as additional home-based Early Intervention services. When Miller turned 3, Jen and Neil wanted him to continue at the Children's Center; however, Miller's home school district felt he should attend their self-contained preschool program for children on the autism spectrum. They proposed that Miller spend the "inclusion part of his day" in a self-contained preschool class-room for children with disabilities but not on the spectrum. Jen remembered very clearly how she felt about this proposal:

> It seemed like a big step backwards after having been at the Children's Center in a classroom with pretty much all typical kids, and then services that he needed being pushed into class for him … I felt in my heart it would be better for him long-term to continue in preschool there and then join our district in kindergarten in a regular class.

Jen convinced the district to allow Miller to stay at the Children's Center through preschool. Looking back now, Jen is sure it was worth the fight:

> I'm positive that was the best thing in the world for him. He was in a room full of kids who were talking, he learned how to talk. You know, it's not the same as someone holding up a flash card. It just isn't. That person holding up that flash card could be the most sincere, committed, and loving person but it does not replace—

I interjected: "It's not as motivating as a peer."
   Jen agreed:

> Yes! And not just one, sixteen peers … all talking! So Miller went to the Children's Center all the way through till he started kindergarten, and then he went to a regular kindergarten class in our district. He had an aide and he still has an aide for part of his day, so he still does need supports. At that time, when he started school there, he was having PT, OT, still needed speech, you know, a lot of supports. But he did beautifully, he did absolutely beautifully because he was accustomed to being around everyone else.

In fact, Miller did so well in kindergarten that the behaviorist that had been working with him felt that he would be able to keep up in first grade without being placed in a classroom co-taught by a special educator. Jen stated that, at the time, this wasn't the right decision for Miller. She explained, that "when kids have what they need in an inclusive setting it looks like they don't need those things, but they still do." After a few weeks, the school principal worked with Jen and Neil to move Miller into a co-taught class.

Even at this young age, Miller demonstrated an awareness of his environment and himself. After a few weeks in his new classroom, he asked his parents if he was going to get "kicked out of the class." Jen explained, "Honey, you didn't get kicked out of class, this other class needed you and so you moved over."

Since then, they have requested that Miller be placed in a co-taught class every year. Jen explained:

> I think it's great to have two teachers in a class and to have flexibility to break up into groups and to have two people looking at someone. He doesn't qualify to be in a co-taught class as an academic qualification for kids who have learning disabilities … he doesn't need it for that, but he needs it to be able to have some flexibility, so I think every year that's where he'll be.

She went on to say, "One disadvantage is all the kids who need extra help are gonna be in his class, so it is less inclusive." But what she appreciates most is the flexibility allowed Miller. For example, when the demands of sitting and attending become challenging, he is free to get up and take a sensory break.

At the time of the interview, Miller was in the sixth grade participating in small groups for only language arts and math. While the curriculum in these classes was modified, he was learning all the same core content. Similar to how Miller's success in kindergarten initially placed him in a first-grade classroom without the support of a special educator, Miller had done so well in math the previous year, that he had been placed in a regular math classroom for sixth grade. Once again, his self-awareness proved a strength. When Jen asked him if he could change anything about his day what it would it be, he said he wanted to go back to the small math class, explaining, "the larger math class is beyond my capabilities." Jen explained, "he's not a person who's like a work avoider … it was just too fast for him … He would kind of day-dream a little bit and then focus back and they had moved right along … So I was very proud of him, though, because he knew, he knew what he needed."

Jen shared that she had the same goal for Mitchell, "for him to be able to know himself enough to know … what he needs for his school and his life, and to be able to express it." She explained that when making decisions for Mitchell and Miller, she asks herself, "What is the most commonsense thing we can do here?" She described offering Miller opportunities to exercise as an example:

> Honestly, I think that if every kid in that class can get up after lunch and exercise for 10 minutes and the teacher too … that everything would be better. It is a universal adaptation that helps everyone … it's not special for somebody with autism.

Jen applies this same "commonsense" approach when considering Miller's social interactions explaining:

> Now his challenge is social interaction and you have to be in class if you're going to have social interaction, you have to be at lunch, you have to be on the playground, instead of being pulled out for something else. I try really to think of an approach that will be the least disruptive to those kinds of things.

Jen added that, in addition to commonsense, flexibility is essential:

> Things can change, that's the thing. And, it's good to try new things ... things don't have to be forever. (For example) Miller's trend over his academic career—when he started in kindergarten, he had lots of supports, then he had fewer and fewer. By third grade ... he didn't need PT, OT and certainly not speech anymore. Then he needed some academic support ... So I can see that needs are dynamic and change all the time.

"I had to really fight, in the nicest and best way that I could."

Jen and Neil's convictions about what would be best for their sons were not always aligned with what professionals were recommending. They reflected on this sometimes trying, and delicate, process:

NEIL: That decision to do due process was painful.
JEN: It was bad.
NEIL: Inside the house, inside here. Should we? Shouldn't we?
JEN: ... The hardest one was pushing for Miller (to stay at the Children's Center). I was working with an advocate at that time and she said, "If you have the stomach to do it, you should tell them that you want to record the meeting."

Jen and Neil did just that, and not only showed up with their tape recorder, but, as Jen explained:

> I had a picture of Miller in front of me 'cause that's who I was doing it for. I was doing it for him and I had to do it in the best way I could for him. I could not lose my cool, you know? And I didn't somehow ... It's very stressful, it's really stressful and worthwhile, you know?

Jen went on to explain some of the nuance involved in the negotiation:

> But then at the same time, there are people sitting around the table with you saying, "Look, you know, he's going to have six kids in class here with him, it's going to be tailored for him, he's going to get so much more attention,"

and that's all true, you know? So it's not like ... they were offering something terrible ... in many ways (it)was a more comprehensive support for him, but I didn't think it was right for him, and I had to really fight, in the nicest and best way that I could, you know, because I did not want to create a bunch of enemies. But they eventually allowed him to continue there.

Jen and Neil can now look back on this stressful time with playful banter:

JEN: They deferred to my wishes eventually ... they deferred to mom, that's what they said.
NEIL: Everyone does, eventually.
INTERVIEWER: Well, you're very charming and persuasive.
NEIL: She's also persistent, persistent as well!

Jen shared that both Mitchell and Miller's current schools enact a very proactive, forward moving philosophy:

The mindset is honestly, what more can we do? What's the next thing we can do? How can we make this a little better? ... It's the culture and I love that, I love that about both the schools ... We have a good match ... it's working very, very, very well.

But this doesn't guarantee that there isn't the potential for different opinions. Jen explains:

For example, about a year and a half ago, Mitchell's school wanted him to start having ... his own nurse that went to school with him. I was completely opposed to this idea ... He needs medical intervention sometimes, but not all day. And, and at most places, if you have a nurse, you don't have ... a one-to-one educational aide ... And so I ended up having to file for due process for him to keep his aide. And so now he has a nurse and an aide. He's the only person at school who does ... It was very stressful and it's also expensive, and I was very concerned that it was going to undermine ... the relationship with (the) school, you know, you're suing them! As it, as it turned out, and I don't know how this could be, but it ultimately was a constructive process ... Our school district sent in a behaviorist to observe Mitchell to see whether he really did need an aide ... And the person did come back and say he ... requires it, he has to have one. And when we all met at the end of it, our director of special services said, I'm really glad that we did this. I feel good that we're providing what he needs ... And it was! ... It took a year, the whole process from start to finish. But I feel very fortunate about that. I can do my part, but you can't do somebody else's part. They have to do their part.

Jen passed along some advice that she had been given:

> it's hard to overstate how stressful and difficult that process is but it's worth doing and it's also worth doing in the most respectful way that you can ... Someone had told me early on that when you have a child with a disability, you are in essence ... married to your school district. You can't burn the bridge down ... you're a team, you know. And so, although it's hard, you have to stay positive and constructive, and it's very hard to do that. It's hard, it is hard to do.

"It changed me and then I reached out more easily to the next person."

Jen described a special connection both she and Miller made with an aide that worked with him at the Children's Center. She had a special affection for Miller and a talent for writing warm, funny notes about his day in his communication notebook. Jen explained:

> I loved to read them and then we started talking, and she was the one that kind of reached beyond like a separate school and home relationship. At first it felt kind of strange to me, but then it was great and so now I do that myself. So, somebody has to be the person to take a little step for those things to happen, for you to really get close and not just be a teacher and student, like to become closer than that. So, I guess for me, once I realized that it was possible to interact that way, it changed me and then I reached out more easily to the next person.

Jen shared other examples of partnerships she'd formed with professionals. One, in particular, was also from when Miller was in preschool. Jen and Neil collaborated with Miller's teacher to choose a challenge that they would work on together. Jen explained what they decided to focus on in this way, "something would happen and he would just kind of fall apart and get upset and then unable to like reset himself." They discussed various techniques to respond to Miller and then sent a video camera back and forth to capture their efforts. Jen recalled:

> And then we sat and looked and talked about like how well it worked, and it allowed us to kind of shape some interventions for him that worked really well ... For a lot of kids, the consistency makes a huge difference ... Tools like that that can help get you on the same page ... I assumed that they're doing things at school the same way that I do them at home, but they're probably not. And there are probably things that are working really well at school that I could do at home.

Jen added that she's currently reaching back to this idea of collaboration and reciprocity as she and Mitchell's teachers work together to increase his participation in his day and his capacity for self-advocacy. She also reflected on times when the collaboration was more strained:

> In Mitchell's first school they just couldn't, really wouldn't, accommodate what he needed. I think it's just like a person. Some people are looking for the way to make something work, you know, like not thinking like why is this hard or what obstacles do we have, but really thinking like what are we gonna need to do to make this work? And once you've encountered someone like that, things just work out. But if someone's looking for things not to work, they don't work. I realized later that his first school underestimated what he was going to need, and then they didn't want to admit that they didn't have what he needed, and so they felt, I think, defensive about it … They were looking to … cover over that they couldn't do what he needed … I'll just be blunt and say that was kind of their focus … not being found out … And honestly not really understanding how to unlock Mitchell's potential either … It just was not a good match.

"So many things!"

When asked what things were going especially well for her family, Jen's immediate and characteristic response was, "So many things!" She followed up commenting, "the most fundamental thing for Mitchell, is his health is good." She explained that the previous summer had been very difficult as Mitchell had been in the hospital four times with seizure activity and over the proceeding months, they had been modifying his medications. She added, that for the last several months "he's been stable and good and that's the most fundamental thing." Jen and Neil explained that there had been years in their family's life that the focus was on "trying to get things … just where everyone's feeling good."

Neil also identified, "health first and foremost … We are not athletic, but we don't have chronic health issues other than Mitchell and his health is stable. So that is a blessing." He went on to explain, "Non-progression of Mitchell's CP … that's important because, at this stage in a child's life with CP as he has it, there would normally be some fairly radical bone surgery with months of recovery. He hasn't had to deal with any of that … So non-progression is a big deal." When I asked to what he would attribute that non-progression, he gave a one-word response: "Feldenkrais." Neil explained, "We do a lot of different kinds of therapy with him and one of them is … called Feldenkrais, and it's named for Moshe Feldenkrais, who invented the therapy." The Feldenkrais Method is described as a type of alternative exercise therapy that can reportedly repair impaired connections between the motor cortex and the body, in order to benefit the quality of body movement and improve overall well-being.

Neil went on to explain, "But he's had a lot of good therapeutic support, and that makes a huge difference too because, like anyone else, if you're not moving, it's really detrimental to every system in your body. Your bones, your muscles, everything! So, for someone in a wheelchair, they have to get out of that chair. They have to move, you know?" Neil reported that they identified a "world-class therapist" with expertise in the Feldenkrais Method. He believes that her work with Mitchell "has kept him from having radical hip surgery for hip dysplasia … So, yes, non-progression!" The B family moved to their current town to be able to access her services, "we are in this house now to be closer to her."

"We're not looking for it to work perfectly. We learn as we go."

Jen shared, "the other thing that really is nice for both boys, they're developing friendships." She went on to describe Miller's last birthday party and her belief that children are learning and demonstrating a new "level of social acceptance":

> There were twenty kids there, and they all had a great time together, and it makes me so happy because one of his challenges is reading social cues … his abilities towards being a friend are improving and part of it is that people are just flexible in how they feel. You know, you don't have to be just one certain way to be a friend, and I can tell that people are learning that at home, you know? And that makes me so happy, that there's just a general level of social acceptance that allows more kinds of people to participate in regular life, you know? So to be able to do that and have fun, and enjoy friends is very, very important.

Both Jen and Neil mentioned Boy Scouts as something else that was going well for both Mitchell and Miller. Jen explained that, while there are troops for people with special needs, they do not belong to those:

> … neither one is so special that they need that much accommodation. We can do what they need … The other thing is they enjoy having … the same experience as everybody else … It doesn't work perfectly, we're not looking for it to work perfectly. We learn as we go. And we're interested and willing to do that.

She went on to describe Mitchell's first camping trip:

> One of the first times they were going to camp as a troop, it was a very cold and rainy weekend, and we were cabin camping … you're still out in the cold but you go into a warm cabin … warmish, you know. We got up in the morning and it was raining and it was cold, and Neil was taking Mitchell, and I said, "Look, if you go for an hour and come home, that's better

than not going, you know? So just go and see what he thinks, and when he's ready to come home, just come home 'cause it's only like forty-five minutes away." Well, he had the best time ... hour after hour went by! He had a slicker on, it quit raining after a while. It warmed up a little bit, not really, and then towards the end of the night, he didn't want to come home, so he spent the night. And it was wonderful!

She added that, even though some of the subsequent camping trips hadn't gone quite as well, they remain committed because, "I want for him to have a bigger variety of experiences and to be able to be with regular people doing regular stuff."

"(Their) schools love and appreciate both of them for who they are."

Jen and Neil are both very satisfied with their sons' current school settings. Jen shared:

> Mitchell's school and Miller's school both love and appreciate both of them for who they are. This is so important, so, so important. My biggest concern mostly for Miller was that someone was going to try to make him into something that he's not, you know, somebody who is able to sit down and be still and look at a board, you know ... I guess he could make himself do that, but not for very long, and it's not who he is.

She explains, "he's learning because people have adapted how they're teaching enough that he is able to do it." She identifies the fact that their teachers are "positive and notice what's going well for them" as vital. Her whole face smiles when she says, "I'll hear things like, 'you know, Miller is so funny, he tells jokes, everyone laughs.' And I'm thinking somebody else might say, 'You know, your son's disruptive' It's all in how you look at it ... I'm so happy that people appreciate Miller for who he is."

Jen shared an example of how Miller's teachers' deep understanding and appreciation of Miller recently allowed them to work together to respond to his behavior in a sensitive, nuanced way:

> During the summer, when Mitchell was in the hospital ... over and over ... four hospitalizations. Miller was actually traumatized by this. I did not realize it at the time, but some really unusual behaviors for him started coming out at school. He started getting upset ... a boy at school was teasing him and he hit him with his water bottle. Like not like horrible things but things that were out of character for him. And even with those things, nobody—everyone helped him. Like they would say, you know, tell us what's going on ... you must not feel like yourself right now. Nobody was upset, you know? ... that's a really great thing to have going well.

INTERVIEWER: They know him, they appreciate him.

JEN: And that if something's wrong, they assume that –

INTERVIEWER: There's a reason for it.

JEN: Yes, and they look for the reason. So those are huge things, huge things.

Jen also recognized that since she and her husband have their own business and work from home, they are more available to participate in school meetings and activities. Neil expressed his appreciation for Miller's school from a different perspective:

> This public school district is amazing. I can't imagine how big the check would have to be for a private school to deliver the kind of … care, attention and variety and just the curriculum that they have here for Miller. They probably just couldn't do it even though private schools focus on one-on-one attention. (This district) is walking the walk. They're just amazing.

"For them to have the same experiences as everyone else is also very important."

Jen and Neil recognize that Mitchell and Miller's education extends beyond the classroom. They explained the ways the four of them reach out to the world around them to share new experiences:

JEN: Last Christmas we went to Disney World. They both absolutely loved it. It was a wonderful family experience. It took a lot of planning when you're traveling with a wheelchair, a gallon of liquid which is what (Mitchell's) food is … the TSA is involved in your flight, everyone's involved … But for them to have the same experiences as everyone else is also very important. For Mitchell's birthday, he went to I Fly, which is that indoor skydiving place. I didn't know if he would enjoy it or not. He's kind of a daredevil and he loved it. But one of the biggest things for them is to keep having experiences where they stretch themselves, like overcome a fear. I would never let them do anything that was like truly dangerous, but there is an element of risk … But it's important to me that they continue having new experiences … it extends your understanding of yourself, you know, that you can do things like that. So, the other things, Mitchell now works out with a personal trainer who is very –

NEIL: Oh, this guy is great.

JEN: … familiar with someone with special needs. It's important … We go to his gym. It's a regular gym, like it's …

NEIL: Muscle heads.

JEN: And so it's important to me that they both have opportunities for health and fitness, and the other thing that's very important is that we do as many of these things in a regular setting with regular stuff as possible. You know, everything has to be adapted, but I want for them both to start having an eye towards that. Like what – as a young adult, what do I need to do to make this work for me?

Jennifer then shared a photo of Mitchell surfing. She and Neil explained that he participated in a volunteer organization called Best Day. Neil went on to describe the day:

NEIL: Oh my God, he loved it. So, every one of these people is a certified life guard and they are taking him out beyond the waves and they're going to surf him in, and they're going to do that three times.
INTERVIEWER: Looks a little scary but exciting.
NEIL: Both. Yeah, you hold your breath as a parent and then you realize, you know what? He might get dunked, but there's six people around him and he's going to be fine, he's going to be fine.

"I can't imagine doing this with someone I butted heads with."

When asked to identify some of the major strengths of their family, Jen and Neil discussed their teamwork:

NEIL: I can't imagine doing this with someone I butted heads with. We do a little –
JEN: a little head butting.
NEIL: A little head butting on Miller … So, I'm the last of four boys, I come from that kind of perspective. Jen is the younger of two girls. So, there's going to be some different opinions. But if you aren't aligned as much as possible, I think you're dead in the water.
INTERVIEWER: With your spouse.
NEIL: … You can't even get out of the gate … We know a few parents who have special needs children who are having problems. And we know a few parents who disagree with typically developing children, and unfortunately, the children bear the brunt of that. So, teamwork is good.

Jen and Neil also identified outside supports that offer their family strength.

NEIL: Outside help is good. I don't think you could possibly come up with all the answers on our own, so we need others to help us out … Not just outside help to give us ideas or to help us like nursing for Mitchell, but also for Miller, he needs to have someone to talk to and we don't hear about it. So, for example, he goes over to the mental health center … twice a week and he talks to Miss Jen over there. I have no idea what they talk about. So, having a variety of outside help I think is super important to make good progress. And money, unfortunately, you either need to have it or be able to find it.

JEN: You have to have enough. You don't have to have a ton, but enough.

NEIL: I think it's fair to say, you know, this is modest, but I can't imagine being able to provide for Mitchell without the state, this state in particular ... because the services here are fantastic. So, either you are able to write your own check or ... you have the curiosity and the determination to dig into, for example, the Division of Developmental Disabilities, the Medicaid waiver, and all those other things that are supplemental aid. If you don't tap into them ... Knowing, researching, penetrating the bureaucracy. Once you get to the right person, he or she is usually helpful. But finding that person, and I'm not saying that I've done it. I know what it's taken for Jen ... It's tough and you need to be curious and have perseverance.

JEN: ... That reminds me ... another group of people that's important to our success is the other moms that I know, and this is also something that's very good about Mitchell's school. They foster parents getting to know one another, and then once you've met people and know them, it's easier to help one another.

INTERVIEWER: You can offer each other a different kind of support than professionals can.

JEN: Yeah, oh definitely ... if you're talking with other people who have a similar situation to yours, you don't have to reinvent the wheel about every single thing ... And also social media, Facebook, things like that ... I'm a member of a moms' group of kids who used to go to (Miller's early childhood program) who still continue to support one another. Like ... there was a little thread going about where there's a sensory-friendly Santa ... those kind of things are also big supports.

"Don't look down."

The conversation about identifying strengths moved from Jen and Neil looking towards each other, to them looking outward into the world, to Neil looking inwardly:

NEIL: Another thing that I think is really important is perspective ... I have a phrase, "Don't look down," and that is my way of saying don't get caught up in comparing. Now I do anyway, and (looking towards Jen) I'm sure you do too, and all special needs parents do ... You know, why did this happen? Why is my son this way and your son is perfect? You can really lose, you can lose your drive, you can lose your perspective. It's a very negative place to dwell. It's impossible not to go there sometimes.

INTERVIEWER: What helps you not look down?

NEIL: Well, first of all, I do ... But getting out of it is, I think, quicker. I'm able to get out of it quicker with a cry, so when I do look down ... I'll go with it. And I will have that mini little Goddammit moment. And then it'll pass and I'll be all right again. But in general, not looking down is realizing that this is a different journey, not necessarily a bad one.

At this point, Neil discussed two stories that help offer him perspective. "Welcome to Holland" a prominent essay, about having a child with a disability written by American author and social activist Emily Perl Kingsley, and a story about an Indian Chief that author, philanthropist, and life coach, Tony Robbins shares. He explains that they're:

> offshoots of don't look down and don't compare … because you don't know what's going to happen to the family that you're comparing against … Avoid it as much as possible because we're, we're dealing with these two, but just down the street in that perfect house, they're dealing with their own and it's a different flavor, but it's just as tough. So that story of maybe, you know, this may be a good thing, this may be a bad thing, but we'll see, and as time goes on, it's going to change. That's what we know: it's gonna change. So don't get too, too mired in, you know, the now because it's going to change.

"We see people at their best."

Neil and Jen went on to reflect that their unique journey has allowed them to intersect with some very special people that they, would otherwise, not have met:

NEIL: Holland is pretty cool … There is an entire universe of people, dimension of people that we would never have known. Now I'm not saying, oh, well, this is worth it. But there are attitude shifts, there are people you meet on this journey that you never would have met if everything were fine.

This reminded me of something Jen had shared with my students when visiting our class:

INTERVIEWER: You said something very similar to that and it made an impact on the class. You said something about … (being) honored, I think was the word you used. That because of the extra help that you need as a family and that Mitchell and Miller need, that you've met all these people and you've gotten to see the best in people.

JEN: It's really true … We see people at their best. We see people extending themselves to help other people every minute. You know, by definition, a nurse in (my) home is there only to help and support someone dear to me, you know. So … if you shift your focus to those things, it's impossible not to feel grateful … The experience we have with people … it's better than most people, it really is … And we also are spending time with people who have chosen helping professions as their life's work. I mean, it's just a different kind of people than working in an office, like I used to. Everyone was nice, it's not that they weren't nice, but it's not the same, you know. When your child's bus driver tells you in her English, which is very clearly her second language, that she's praying for your son every night as if he were her own, she means that … it's so touching, you know, that someone would care enough about your child that not only is she keeping him safe on the bus, but she is including him –

INTERVIEWER: She's carrying him home with her.

JEN: Yes. And … it's really beautiful.

NEIL: It's humbling as well.

JEN: It is humbling … And also it inspires me to try to do my best for other people however I can … And believe me, I don't do it all the time, I don't do it as often as the people who come into our house do, but I try my best like to do something at a minimum to let those people know that what they're doing matters, you know? Because I think people who live that way need to hear that the things that they're doing matter and to do something to say thank you.

After sharing many examples of seemingly small things that professionals have done for her family that have made a very big impact, Jen added:

And again, like you were saying, would I trade all of these great things for our kids to be up walking and doing? Yes, I would! But you know, my life is considerably better, you know, and different in a much better way because of this, because of our situation …

"That he's still able to be kind of funny and a little off center, and find his way happily."

Jen and Neil had a lot to share when asked about their goals and dreams for Mitchell and Miller. Neil's response was thoughtful and specific:

For Miller, it's acceptance, and for him to find his way and be happy and productive with his quirks. But also, where he matures … and the eventual teasing of his social skills does happen. I hope it doesn't squash him and that he's still able to be kind of funny and a little off-center and find his way happily. That would be great. For Mitchell, my eventual hope is some degree of rehabilitation through either stem cells or gene therapy to reactivate part of the brain that was hurt and maybe regrow some connections there. That would be terrific. Beyond that, if that doesn't happen, then safety and a caring environment as close to … what we provide for him ourselves will be provided for him when we can't and when we're gone … a safe place, a comfortable place, and with people who care. They don't have to love him like we do, but I would like him to be cared for beyond the perfunctory, overly sterile, hygienic places ...

Jen also shared her goals and dreams for Mitchell and Miller and her hopes for how they'll contribute to the world around them:

> My hope for Miller is that his unique perspective and abilities will find ... a direction for him to ... contribute to the world. He really is unique. He is so funny. He is observing everything, he's putting things together in his way ... I really, I'm excited for him because I think the world has changed enough that people who are not marching along in the same way are valued. I don't know what he's going to do, but he is a master at building things, like making games, engaging people and playing, and he has some very special gifts and I hope that they find their path, you know, for him to be able to do something unique in the world. And for Mitchell, for him, I hope that more of who he is can become known to other people ... They're both unique people and I know that, from the little glimpses of what he's thinking about ... He can give us some clues from his communication device and the things he pays attention to and enjoys, that more of those things will be out where people can see them, you know?

Jen explained how technology will play a lasting role in not only Mitchell's ability to communicate but also in his ability to access educational opportunities and be included in the community:

> ... Whatever kinds of things it is, genetics, testing, gene therapy, stem cells, whatever kinds of things are only going to improve his situation, allow him to communicate more the same way that that device does ... I remember when not long after he got his Tobii, he and Miller were playing up in the family room and ... Miller didn't want to play with him, and he told me his feelings were hurt. Like I wouldn't have known that, I wouldn't have known it by looking at his face, and that's a tiny example, but his world is going to be unlocked so much more by things that are yet to be discovered, developed, you know. He's fifteen. When he's thirty-five, it'll be a different world. Probably when he's twenty-five, it'll be a different world, you know? And I'm excited for him for that. Fifteen or twenty years ago, a much smaller disability than he has would have excluded him from probably an education ... being in Boy Scouts, you know, the attitudes have changed. Technology has changed, people's ideas about what's possible have changed, and they will continue to change. And that will only make things better for him ... I say this to Mitchell all the time and it is true, that medical

technology and other kinds of technology are going to be his friend his whole life, you know

As Jen glimpses into his future, she considers how Mitchell can contribute to the world:

> And that he'll have his own impact in the world with more people … My hope is that the place we're creating for him to live will become not only a place where he will live and enjoy his life with his friends … (but also) will become something that other people can also duplicate for their own families. Not only their young kids, it could be for their elderly parents, it could be for anyone who needs that kind of help. But I really think … that they're here because they have something that they need to do and, and that they're supposed to do, and I really hope that I can support them in doing that. But I really think they both have a reason for being here. Or they wouldn't be here.

Jen and Neil share a warm exchange about the affection that Mitchell and Miller stir in others:

JEN: Mitchell somehow inspires tremendous love and –
NEIL: Loyalty.
JEN: loyalty in people … And I make this joke, actually, it's not a joke, but I used to think that people liked Mitchell and Miller because Neil and I were great people … but … I remember the day clearly when I realized that was actually not the case. (laughs) It really was that people liked us because of our children, you know?
INTERVIEWER: They're the real ambassadors.
JEN: Yeah, they are! They really – and people have even said it overtly. One of the first people we had come into our house to help with Mitchell said … I love Mitchell so much and you two are okay too. That's what she said! … She was a tell it like it is kind of person, and I realized that it was not us, you know. That people like us because they had gotten to know Mitchell and Miller. But it really is true.

"Some empathy is good, but sympathy is not."

Jen and Neil talked about the kinds of reactions that they receive from others and what they'd like them to understand about Mitchell and Miller and their family. Neil started with:

> I always say, 'don't blame them … don't blame them for the things you think are easily correctable.' For example … behavior things. 'Why can't you just?' … You know. I have to remind myself of that …

INTERVIEWER: Is that something you bump into, that you feel people do sometimes, blame them?

NEIL: Well, yeah, yeah, because I only said that because I've blamed them both myself. But then you realize how utterly nonsensical that is. So, I'm assuming that if I have felt it, other people have felt it ... 'cause it's an easy thing to do, it's an easy scapegoat. But you can't unload that monkey, I'm sorry, you just cannot ... Acknowledgment and maybe some empathy is good, but sympathy is not.

INTERVIEWER: How would you make that distinction?

NEIL: Okay. 'Bless your heart' is not necessary. 'Oh, you're so strong. How do you do that?' No. No. That's sympathy and that's syrup, and it's well-meaning because people have to say something ... Some sort of acknowledgment, but that ain't it. Another no is, 'Oh, I could never do that.' Well, yes, you can, yes, you can, because if you had to, you would. So treating parents of special needs just like anybody else, and that's what our friends do. They accommodate Mitchell. When we go over to their home and they don't have a ramp, they help me pick him up. They acknowledge and accommodate. They don't cater and they don't overdo it. And that's the best thing to do. You move on, you may have to slow down the fleet because you've got a ship that doesn't move as fast, but you still move right along.

INTERVIEWER: You're still part of the fleet.

NEIL: Still part of the fleet, yeah. We are not going to be on time ... And rib us for it, but don't get mad. All right?

Both Neil and Jen felt that, overall, "people in general, and kids especially, have come a long way in terms of not making fun, accommodating ... you know, people in wheelchairs, they're just not as shunned as they used to be."

INTERVIEWER: What do you attribute that to, that change?

NEIL: ADA. (The Americans with Disabilities Act) Two things. One is, I think, more people in chairs are coming out. It started with marathons and people in chairs doing stuff, inserting themselves into regular society. And then parents doing it as well with their children. So the athletes who may have had an accident and then decided, I'm going to play basketball in a wheelchair ... I think they were on the vanguard. The ADA helped an awful lot.

JEN: Also ... more people being in school, because IDEA (Individuals with Disabilities Act) helped a lot too, that people, everyone being in school – I don't know about you, but there was nobody in a wheelchair in my school ... Well, it's funny, it seems to me being kind is overtly taught at school now ... I think it's a great thing ... I see, when I see Miller talking to friends at school ... even though his conversation topics are a little different, you know, people just kind of go with it. They accept him for who he is for the most part.

This idea of embracing and building up from differences echoes a definition of inclusion that Jen offered during an interview I conducted with her for a previous study:

> It really, to me, is using the strengths of a group of different people together to teach everyone … Because everyone in the classroom, everyone has special abilities and gifts and also difficulties and so it is … it really is an approach where someone is looking for those things within each person that can help every-one … we could harness so much more of people's abilities and talents.

"They are a piano recital."

Neil and Jen are able to recognize their own accomplishments as parents:

NEIL: I think we're doing a pretty good job. Mitchell is not regressing, and is in many ways progressing, it is glacially slow, but he is progressing. And both boys are happy … when they wake up in the morning, they're optimistic. (pause) It scares the hell out of us for when we're not here, but that's a different topic.

JEN: I feel good about the fact that we are doing everything we can. You know, we are committed … and, I mean like a hundred percent committed. Because that is actually what it takes … I think the other thing that's important really is perseverance, like being able to stick with something for as long as it takes because sometimes it can take a really long time, you know, for things to bear fruit … for example, Mitchell's … communication device. It took probably a good five or six years, for him to really start using it in a basic way … You have to train yourself to look for the small improvements.

NEIL: You've got to look, you've got to reset your expectations. And be aware of the little gains.

JEN: And to focus on those … Actually, honestly, to celebrate those, as if they were a piano recital or – 'cause they are, that's what they are! They are a piano recital.

Neil also described acknowledging the smaller things:

> Like when Miller comes home with his paper clip on the highest level of the clip chart, he's in sixth grade, he still uses a clip chart because it's very tan-gible and he likes it. So, when he comes home on 'great job', man, he gets a hug so hard! … it's a constant game of readjusting expectations. That's the biggest thing for me, readjusting expectations.

"It's a boldness, that's what it is."

Jen explained that, as a parent, she's learned that she's able to apply her own enthusiasm and vision to assembling and motivating groups of professionals to work together in support of her sons. She also recounted how, from her very first days as a parent, she learned to trust her own judgment:

> From the very, very start, I remember when this happened actually. Mitchell was in the NICU, he was a newborn and they were trying to decide whether he was going to be able to eat or not, like take a bottle … he wasn't organized very well to swallow and … his gag reflex wasn't normal and it may not be safe, you know? And one day we came into the NICU and a nurse was giving him a bottle, and I thought to myself, 'Wow, that's so great, he's having a bottle.' And then like a second later, I felt something like roar up in me, like who said it was okay for him to have that bottle? I'm going to find out—and I realized like it was my job, like it wasn't just okay to like let somebody else make a decision and be okay with that … But I realized, and it was just in a flash, that that was my role to step in, question things, not just accept what other people said. I mean, what if that was a mistake? Like what if he wasn't supposed to be having that and someone didn't read the chart, you know? But there's nothing that will replace a parent's role like that, and especially, honestly a Mom's role, like to step in, question things, get things organized, motivate people to help. Like it's, it's an expanded role. It was not the role I thought I'd be having. But … I get to do that all the time, you know? Honestly, to ask for Mitchell to have a nurse and an aide … when I said it, it seemed preposterous. Nobody else had that, you know? … People are probably like, well, yeah, that would be great. We don't do that! So, but to be the person that decides that that is, in fact, what needs to happen … It's a boldness, that's what it is.

INTERVIEWER: Boldness. That's a good word.

JEN: And it's different to think boldly than it is to act boldly because people can see you acting boldly, you know? … I would like this year for Mitchell to start being in our local school for at least part of his day … I can tell you when I mention this idea, everyone's mouth is going to fall open. Our school district's gonna go, oh my God, we can't do that … But they can, they just need to reorganize themselves and …

INTERVIEWER: And act more boldly.

JEN: Yes! … But it never ends, we are working actively on a place for Mitchell to live when he is an adult, you know? Same thing. It's inventing something, it's being courageous enough to do that and not just accept what's available … So it actually feels great to think about things like that. It's also a little scary, you know, and you have to have enough confidence in what I'm saying to, to move ahead, you know? But … I wouldn't want to live any other way. Why would you want to live in a way where you're not acting boldly, and just accepting what other people think is best.

"Big waves."

Neil and Jen look at their experience and consider how they would translate it into advice they would share with other parents.

NEIL: A piece of advice I would give to a new parent who is dealing with this is you can't part-time this. And you also can't live two lives. You can't live the life you thought you were going to live, – sorry, you're not gonna go out with the guys as much or at all. As soon as you can internalize and deal with that, do it, because if you're going to be a good parent to your now special needs child, you just, you can't run away from this. If you do, you will drown in the guilt and your child will just wallow. So, the faster you can wrap your head around what you have, not just from a diagnosis and a prognosis point of view, but a what does this mean to me, my dashed hopes and what I need to do going forward, the better. And it's an ongoing process. It's not, Oh, I'm there. I finally figured it out. Now I'm perfectly aligned with saying goodbye to all of that.

JEN: The biggest piece of advice I would give anyone is to enjoy your children, honestly, for who they are … at every age, you know, an infant, a toddler, a four-year-old, a grade schooler, all have their charms and appeal, and to focus on that as much as possible while you're also focusing on helping them

They also had advice to share with professionals and teachers in training:

JEN: The most important thing, I think, is to look for the positives and to communicate the positives. Anyone who is in special education, any child in special education by definition has got some challenges, and the parents are well aware of – I think it's even more important if it's someone whose child has a lot of difficulty, like if they have a lot of behavioral issues or they have a lot of difficulty even being in class, you know? If there's something good that happens, to report about that because it plants a seed of hope, you know, and it also, I think, can change the way that someone interacts with their child, if they feel hopeful, you know? … And also give you something to talk about with your child at home, you know, that's not just how was school today. So, it could be, it could be any kind of an accomplishment. The first day that Miller peed on the potty, like it was … a very big day … and I got a whole note home about that. It was a great thing … Now, like when Mitchell has an especially communicative day with his Tobii, I hear the entire conversation, you know, so that's above and beyond.

NEIL: As a professional gains experience and sees twenty Mitchells and thirty Mikes and forty Allisons and each one becomes less special because … the individual starts to get lost as the pace of the professional's day gets faster.

And it's easy to start looking at the diagnosis and ... So to check in as often as needed to make sure that you're still talking to and thinking about each child as an individual.

JEN: I would just add one more thing and this is so important to me. To not be afraid ... as a teacher, to reach out to a parent and say something like, I'm not sure how to help your child ... Here is what I've tried. Do you have some ideas? Not to be afraid to collaborate ... Say something right away, you know?

At the end of our interview, Jen and Neil reflected on their experiences in the following way.

JEN: But there's been a lot ... it's a high-seas kind of parenting. Like there's a lot of –
NEIL: HA! Yes. Big waves, big waves.
JEN: Big ones, you know ... but you know what? It's also, it's exciting because we're not bored, we're not bored.

Questions for Discussion

1. How would you describe the B family's strengths and resources?
2. How does this family work together to support their children and each other?
3. How would you characterize the B family's communication and collaboration with professionals?
4. In Jen's definition of inclusion, she promotes "using the strengths of a group of different people together to teach everyone" as a way to "harness so much more of people's abilities and talents." Consider how, as a teacher, you can enact these tenets in your classroom as well as promote them in community experiences.
5. In this family's story, we can see how educational, medical, and technological needs and resources are integrated. Discuss the potential challenges and opportunities that interdisciplinary collaboration may present in serving children and families.

7

A FAMILY REFLECTS ON THEIR ACHIEVEMENTS AND DREAMS

My time with the Morrobel family, which spanned over two visits and totaled more than four hours, didn't feel as much like an interview as a friendly visit. They unanimously agreed to participate in the process as a group, rather than separately, and they were each engaged, thoughtful, and animated throughout. For a majority of our time together, I felt like instead of participating in a conversation with the four of them, I was facilitating a conversation between them. It was fascinating to spend time with this family and to witness their warm interactions and vivid insights.

I was introduced to the Morrobel family by friends who had previously visited my class as guest speakers; they knew each other through the New Jersey State Deaf-Blind Project and the National Family Association for Deaf-Blind. They had visited my class on three separate occasions over the previous two years. We sat together at a big dining table: Pam, Angel (who goes by Carlito), Ethan, 16 at the time, and Gavin, just a few days away from his 14th birthday.

Ethan and Gavin have Usher Syndrome, a genetic disease that causes hearing loss, vision loss, and difficulties with balance. Ethan was diagnosed with profound sensorineural hearing loss at 10 months and Usher Syndrome at 7 years old. Gavin was diagnosed with sensorineural hearing loss at birth and Usher Syndrome at 5 years old. Both Ethan and Gavin have bilateral cochlear implants. Ethan was first "implanted" at 13 months and Gavin at 8 months. Due to their visual impairment, Retinitis Pigmentosa, each of the boys was registered legally blind.

"We're from everywhere, basically."

Our conversation started with a discussion about how they define their race or ethnicity. After a lively exchange about some of the novel, nuanced information they had recently received from Ancestry.com, they each settled on the following definitions:

Carlito explained that he was "born here, but both my parents are Dominican. But ... Dominican is such a mixture, so we had also a seven to nine percent Senegal, which is where my dark skin comes from ..."

ETHAN: We're from everywhere, basically.
PAM: Which is kind of cool 'cause I identify firmly as Canadian. Firmly, firmly.
INTERVIEWER: And how about the rest of you? How do you identify firmly? (laughs)
CARLITO: Latino, I guess.
INTERVIEWER: Okay. How about you guys?
GAVIN: Canadian American.
ETHAN: Canadian Dominican.
PAM: Yeah, 'cause he was born in the Dominican.
CARLITO: So he's the only Dominican.
GAVIN: I was born in Canada.
CARLITO: So he's Canadian and American and Ethan has all three.

These distinctions prompted me to ask them to recount their journey as a family.

PAM: We started as a family in the Dominican Republic. We met down there and we got married down there ... I was teaching in Canada and wanted to get a teaching job somewhere warm ... So my first job I got was at an international school in the Dominican Republic, and his brother-in-law was the principal ... And we lived there for seven years ... we got married in '99 ... And he (Ethan) was born in 2001 ... And we discovered he was deaf in ... October 2002, and that's when we made arrangements to move to Canada.
CARLITO: Well, we went first to Miami. He got his first implant, his first surgery ... We rented a house in Miami and we were flying back and forth. There were not a lot of other people with cochlear implants in the Dominican. We didn't have anybody qualified for audio-verbal therapy and all the other stuff that we needed to do. So, at that point, we knew we had to move.
PAM: And the one thing they told us is that we need to stay in the maternal language, and we were surrounded by Spanish in the Dominican Republic. That is not true anymore, but based on what they knew then, that's what they told us.
CARLITO: So, no sign, no Spanish, no French, nothing.
PAM: ... we considered moving to Miami, we considered moving to many different areas in the States, and we went with New Brunswick, Canada, which was my hometown, for the family support ...
CARLITO: Yeah, and I quit my job. They didn't want to let me go so I kept staying a few more weeks and a few more weeks until finally I said, 'Look, I gotta go.' And then one of ... the vice presidents heard that I had quit and asked where I was going, and I said I was going to Canada. So we had an

office in Toronto, the company, that was not doing well and they were thinking of closing it, and so he offered me a position up there.

PAM: And so then, somehow (laughs) along the way, I get pregnant ... So that changed everything, and we packed up, Ethan and I (laughs), eight months pregnant, and moved to Toronto ... And we discovered soon after that Gavin was deaf and that settled things. We were staying in Toronto. So we lived there for ten years.

INTERVIEWER: What brought you here?

PAM: They approached him a few times about moving, but I always said no, we need to worry about them, language, you know, therapy ... we didn't know about Usher Syndrome yet, but we still had them in all the different therapies that you would for that because we knew something was happening ... so we didn't want to move. But then ... after ten, eleven years ... they came to him with another job offer to move to New Jersey, and he came home thinking that I was just going to nip it in the bud and say no. But I was thinking about all their needs and I'm working full-time and all the things I'm doing, I just didn't have time for it anymore. And I thought, well, if we can go, if this job like jumps you up so I don't have to work full-time anymore, then let's do it. And along the way, our goal with them was always to just experience life ... So we thought this would be another great experience for them, and we got together as a family and discussed it 'cause we weren't going to do it unless they were willing to.

Ethan and Gavin were 9 and 12 at that time. They remembered their reactions to the possibility:

ETHAN: At the time, I wasn't that much like into politics and, you know, all that kind of stuff ... it was just, oh ... the States, and so it was just something different. And then she said New York City, because we were going to be like forty minutes away.

INTERVIEWER: And so, what did that mean when you heard New York City?

ETHAN: I was like, that's cool. (laughs) Like I'm down ... Yeah, my twelve-year-old brain just went crazy.

INTERVIEWER: How about your nine-year-old brain?

GAVIN: I wasn't sure what to think about it ...

ETHAN: I think we all had a consensus on the adventure part, where it's just like something new. It was difficult to leave our friends, but we were like (clap) adventure.

GAVIN: I just thought it would be cool to like be able to go to New York.

The four of them reminisced about some of the "cool" things they do as a family in New York City, especially when they have friends and family visiting. Their list included Yankee games "especially when the Bluejays are there," Times

Square, Little Italy, Chinatown, the Statue of Liberty, the Empire State Building, and a special memory of skating in Central Park at midnight.

"I have left little pieces of me in a lot of cities."

When asked how they would define their family, they each had different responses. Gavin identified the four of them and their dog, Erickson. Ethan prefaced his response with "My answer's a lot longer than that." He also started out with the five of them, and then moved on to include "everyone" from his mother's and father's side of the family. Next he added his "four guy friends" and their immediate family members, and two families that have merged the titles of friends and family for all of them. When I inquired what he considered when deciding "who makes the cut," he had a very clear response, "I just think about people who really support my Usher Syndrome and just are really supportive of me in general."

Carlito also began with "this nucleus right here" and then moved on to explain,

> I've been fortunate in my life, and even though I have lived in many places and moved around a lot, I feel like I have left little pieces of me in a lot of cities ... But, I would say (pause) besides Pam's family and my family, outside of us, then I have a core group of friends that we've been together since fourth grade ... it doesn't matter (pause) how far apart we've been ... it's like time doesn't pass ... you can always go back to that core and they're always there.

He went on to explain one way they maintain their friendships:

CARLITO: Every time we go to the D.R. (Dominican Republic), we also try to throw a little get-together because it's easier to be in one place and say, 'Hey, people, come over' ... it's always nice.
PAM: If you throw a party, they'll come.
INTERVIEWER: It sounds like you have a lot of people that love you in different places.

Carlito expanded his answer to include, "our family at Sick Kids ... that's the hospital in Toronto ... Because we spent so much time there and we went through so much together ..." Pam quickly added with a laugh, "You stole my answer!" Carlito, Pam and Ethan all joined in to describe the enduring relationships they had formed with the professionals including doctors, audiologists, social workers, receptionists and "the whole team." Pam shared that when they returned to visit after four years, "everybody knew we were coming and everybody came to see us!"

Ethan included as part of their "Sick Kids family" another family that they met when Ethan and their son had their second cochlear implants. They continue to visit each other in New Jersey and Toronto and enjoy going skiing together. Pam made a distinction in her definition of family:

I'm more of a traditionalist, so I'm always like family is family ... Like my brothers and sisters and my aunts and uncles and my parents, and his side of the family. And because I'm a twin, I have that relationship with her, so that's sustained me for so long. But wherever we've been, we've always tried to (pause) establish people, like ex-pats, that they don't have any family either, so we make arrangements. We get together all the holidays and so we, we've been doing that here too. So that's loosely defined as family.

"it only works if both sides buy in."

Pam explained that contributing to the connections they made with the staff at Sick Kids was the fact that they knew them "from the beginning." She described their family-centered approach:

> ... we went for the longest time as a family ... They didn't make decisions for us. We sat as a group and made decisions, and the award that I nominated them for was for family-centered care. Two awards actually. And they did win both of them. So, it was just that everybody was involved.

Pam reminisced about the skating and summer events that they held for staff and families to spend time together and laughed remembering how at one of the events, they "made a cochlea out of people" capturing it with a photo from above. She explained that they haven't been able to recreate this kind of partnership with other programs and professionals. Ethan and Carlito joined Pam in her attempt to identify the distinct elements that fostered their family-centered approach:

CARLITO: I think the difference is, it's not (pause) a client-based kind of medicine where you come in, you get fixed, and you go. It was more in order for you to get fixed, the whole family needed to be involved in a way because that is how you need to –
ETHAN: You need the support.
CARLITO: Exactly. That's how the (cochlear) implant will work and, and the education of ...
PAM: And Dad needs to know what's going on too ... not just Mom.
CARLITO: And ... if they were around, like the grandparents or the aunts or the uncles because ... it helps to have everybody involved and know so they could be as successful as they are. That's the way I saw it.
PAM: ... that was their goal, but the family has to buy into it too and that's that blog that I wrote ... our audio-verbal therapist has a website so I wrote this blog for her, ten suggestions ... on good professional family relationships ... 'cause it's our job too.

Pam explained that one of their strategies was to make sure the days that they went to their appointments were made special:

> we would make sure that ... we'd make it a fun day, so we'd have our appointment but we'd go do something fun ... go to the museum ... the aquarium, or ... our favorite food truck ... When they were young, if I bought them an airplane, that was enough. We had a huge collection of airplanes 'cause they were like what are we going to get, we're going to Sick Kids. So they went in with excitement!

Pam and Carlito went on to explain how they made a conscious effort to build relationships with the professionals at Sick Kids:

PAM: ... we would tell them personal information about the boys, they started to know us more as people ... it only works if both sides buy in
CARLITO: You have to be genuine ...
PAM: Yeah, and they just liked talking to people. Yeah, you guys just always just liked going to places and doing things ... Maybe it's 'cause we always did that.

The Cochlear Implant Team at Sick Kids did buy in! They created an environment that welcomed the Morrobels, and, as Pam explained, "they became part of our family." Also, the idea that they like talking to people, going to places, and doing things rang especially true to me. Each time the Morrobel family visits my class, they are open and enthusiastic and leap into my students' hearts! In fact, on more than one occasion, Gavin has accomplished this feat by way of demonstrating a back flip!

"we had to own it for them until they're old enough to learn it for themselves."

They shared another example of how their open natures created an opportunity to build a meaningful partnership with professionals. While attending a Broadway performance, Carlito struck up a conversation with a gentleman who noticed the boys' cochlear implants and shared that his wife worked for an agency that served children with implants. They exchanged contact information and soon developed a relationship that included the agency conducting the boys' hearing and language assessments and the Morrobel family participating in the agency's fundraising efforts including playing in a golf tournament and speaking at the event.

Carlito explained their open approach in this way: "... Pam and I ... from day one was there's no shame, and we feel like the kids are innocent and when they're growing up, you pass on the shame if you have (it)."

Gavin and Pam joined in to explain what they think makes the difference:

GAVIN: I'd say it's definitely more on the parents' part because let's say we had parents who didn't want it, that means we couldn't do it without their support and their help because ... they wouldn't be able to bring us places, you know what I mean? We couldn't drive or anything like that, so I really say it's how the parents deal with it. So I feel like we're very fortunate to have parents that try to help as much as possible ... like the parents act, that will carry on to the children, so then that will affect how the children act, so each is like a chain from there.

PAM: ... it's just (pause) it's a difference between wanting to fix your child and being, I guess –

CARLITO: Supportive.

PAM: just who they are, you know ... given the culture that he (Carlito) grew up in, he's very unusual in the way that he dealt with it compared to what many of his friends or family would.

This led to a discussion of Pam and Carlito's teamwork:

PAM: I think we agreed early on we would go to our strengths. You trust me for the education and that aspect of what we need to do, like move to Canada, and I'll trust you in doing the research for technology and what's the best up-to-date thing ... And it wasn't about fixing them, it was about how can we help them become the best that they can be, which you do for your children anyway. You just got a few extra things to have to tweak.

CARLITO: ... what I like to think is we wouldn't have done anything any different (pause) without the condition or with the condition ... I would have played ball with them and everything else that I've done the same way ... you gotta own it and they have to own it and we had to own it for them until they're old enough to learn it for themselves.

He went on to explain:

... As a child, I don't remember many handicapped kids in the Dominican, but by the numbers you know that they were there. But it was kind of almost like they were hidden ... that was one of our things from day one ...

As an example, Pam and Carlito shared that instead of trying to hide the boys' cochlear implants, they let them pick out fun "skins" or covers for them that made them stand out.

Pam also explained the conscious decision they made to engage the boys in their own advocacy:

... the number one thing we decided early on was they need to start advocating for themselves early, so they started speaking to people you know, taking the cochlear coloring books and presenting everything to their class.

They started that early, and then moved to teaching, to speaking at workshops for teachers who were going to have hearing impaired children in the class, and then going to universities …

Ethan and Gavin were even featured on a show on Canadian television. Currently, as part of their advocacy efforts, they are Student Ambassadors for Ava's Voice, an organization that aims to empower youth with Usher Syndrome.

Gavin reflected on an interaction he had with a classmate after one of his class presentations:

GAVIN: … I remember I talked about my disability and all that, and then one of my classmates … came up to me (and said) they had something that they didn't really … accept or liked very much and that my presentation inspired them to … accept who they are. So I remember that, and then I also remember that I'm helping other people out who will help other people who are like me … so I'm happy …

INTERVIEWER: That's certainly what you're doing when you come to my class … You're speaking to people that are going to be teachers.

"you lend yourself to be, let's not say loved, but liked."

Ethan jumped into the conversation to announce, "We forgot about teachers!" This led to a review of the many "school teachers" and "teachers of the deaf" they had had over the years. The following highlights from this portion of the conversation demonstrate the things they valued in their teachers and the way they continue to carry them with them.

ETHAN: I had her for two years, she was the best teacher ever.

PAM: She asked to teach the next grade so she could have you again.

ETHAN: Yeah, it was great, and –

PAM: You loved her. (whispers) He loved her.

ETHAN: … I just I remember really being happy with her as my teacher … but then there was also my teacher of the deaf … she always took us out of the class once a week for like thirty minutes and it was always the thirty minutes I was looking forward (to) …

INTERVIEWER: What kinds of things did you do with (her)?

GAVIN: We played games.

ETHAN: There was the actual stuff we had to do, like the hearing tests and all that kind of stuff, but then if we were done with that, we'd just talk.

GAVIN: Just play games.

ETHAN: Play games. She's the one that actually got me into politics. (laughs)

PAM: Current events, yeah, you guys talking (about) the world, we'd get a map because we were always doing that at home too.

GAVIN: And then one of the things we did … before we knew we were going to move … she would always play games with us about Canada and show us the Rocky Mountains … but then once we got closer to moving, she would always bring maps of New York and New York City, the United States and everything like that, and it was just always fun and helpful to have her around …

Pam explained, that while she acknowledges current practice tends to endorse "push in" services, she also values the unique advantages of pull-out services. She drew on her own work as a special educator as well as Ethan and Gavin's experiences:

PAM: I strongly believe in pull-out; I think it's unfortunate that we're going in a different direction because I believe we need a continuum of services.

Ethan explained that he was worried that after they moved, it would be difficult to find a teacher that could compare. But in describing their next teacher, he and Gavin shared:

ETHAN: She was just as good, she was, she was great as well. We did the stuff we needed to do and we talked.
GAVIN: We'd play games.

There were also a few teachers that they remembered less fondly:

PAM: There was one time where we had somebody which neither of you guys liked. (laughs) I didn't like … She had no personality, you know what I mean?
ETHAN: Yeah, she was just very general. She wanted to do this stuff and then if we finished early, I went back to class, you know, it wasn't fun.

Pam and Carlito explained how they foster strong partnerships with teachers:

PAM: I would make sure and meet with the teachers and talk about them and what their interests were and how they needed, really needed to be involved …
CARLITO: I think it goes back to the same as the hospital staff … it comes from both sides, but they engage with people. In Spanish we say se dan a querer which is, you lend yourself to be (pause) let's not say loved, but liked.

Ethan and Gavin have aides that accompany them during their school day. They have very clear ideas about the delicate balance that an aide needs to strike to be supportive but not intrusive. They explained the importance of communicating with their aides to ensure that they understood their needs for both support and independence. When asked what makes a good aide, Gavin explained it like this:

GAVIN: Well, easy-going for sure ... mine was perfect. So basically, like she was really easy-going ... she didn't step in unless ... she knew that I needed ... something. And she was always kind of out of the way ... let's say I wanted to walk in the hallways a bit separately from her because I just wanted to be with my friends and all that, and she could do that perfectly fine.

ETHAN: ... It's more than just them being your aide, it's them being your –

PAM: They're being their eyes and their ears and a lot.

ETHAN: Basically, almost your friend ...

CARLITO: ... I would compare her to a caddy ... When you play golf with a caddy, he knows when you hit a shot, before you even think, he's like here's the club.

INTERVIEWER: So, what would you say are the top three things you want in an aide?

GAVIN: Easy-going ... Nice. Well, obviously like nice ... Friendly, like easy to talk to, kind of like that kind of easy vibe, just like very friendly, like an elementary school teacher.

Pam's own vast experience as an educator makes her uniquely qualified to communicate and collaborate with teachers. Over her career as an educator in New Brunswick, the Dominican Republic, Toronto, and now New Jersey, Pam has worked as a first, third, fifth, sixth, and seventh grade general education teacher. She also worked as a Middle School and High School Special Education Resource Teacher and as a Special Education Transition Teacher for students 19–21 years old. Carlito spoke proudly about Pam's work:

CARLITO: And in that last one, they still miss you. She connected with all those kids, some kids that were unreachable and she reached them ... I know they still miss you over there ...

INTERVIEWER: They're talking about you the way these guys are talking about some of their teachers.

PAM: And some of the parents ... I still have connections with because I would try to do things outside ... the one thing I always said is I wasn't going to be a hypocrite and we listened to everything the doctors said 'cause ... as a special ed teacher, I was always like, 'Why aren't people listening to the recommendations in the report, right?' They're not just there for fun. This is what you need to do. So we followed pretty much every recommendation.

ETHAN: Half was good, half was bad.

INTERVIEWER: On recommendations?

ETHAN: Yes, half, like the half good obviously, therapy and all that kind of stuff, and then half bad is like not learning the ASL.

PAM: Oh yeah, yeah, if we could go back –

CARLITO: Yeah, we would have done (it).

Pam described how she establishes a connection with Ethan and Gavin's teachers:

PAM: And I always send an email ... from the beginning of the year, thanking them in advance, and saying, I know my children have IEPs, no one's going to remember everything, I forget things, but I look forward to working together and figuring out along the way these are the most important things to remember about them, the most important accommodations will be this ... And start with a greeting, hope everything's well, thanks for everything you do for my children, just wanted to check in about this.

"and then half bad is like not learning the ASL."

The conversation returned to the topic of ASL (American Sign Language). As the Morrobel family looks back, they characterize the recommendation they had received from professionals that they not learn it as belonging in the category "bad recommendations": "and then half bad is like not learning the ASL." Ethan had recently attended a week-long camp hosted by the National Technical Institute for the Deaf. In his description of his time there, he uses the terms "Capital D Deaf" and "lower-case d deaf." In general, Deaf (with a capital D) refers to people who identify themselves as culturally deaf and have a strong deaf identity that includes embracing the cultural norms, beliefs, and values of the Deaf Community. In contrast, deaf (with a lower-case d) refers to the medical condition of having hearing loss. People who identify as deaf often don't have a strong connection to the Deaf community and most likely do not use sign language, preferring to communicate orally. This is often the case when individuals have been born to hearing parents and grown up in the hearing world with little or no exposure to the Deaf community.

ETHAN: I went a month ago almost. There was a camp for capital D Deaf and lower-case d deaf ... going into junior year and going to senior year kids ... And it was just a camp about learning about what you want to do in college, and it was a chance for me to meet a lot of people, other deaf people as like a lower-case d deaf person, I met a lot of the first capital D Deaf people I've ever met.

Ethan referred to a TV show I was familiar with, *Switched at Birth,* that dealt with some of the nuanced issues of the deaf and Deaf communities and the controversial topic of cochlear implants. He and Pam described the impact his time at camp had on him.

ETHAN: ... I've loved that show and so I was afraid at first about going in. I was like am I going to be the only person with technology? And I was worried about the view that the other people were going to have on me, 'cause like in the show, it shows that they have a negative view. And so it was funny because ... I was one of the first people that got there, I was playing outside and all of the capital D Deaf people were outside playing sports with me. All the lower-case d deaf people were inside just talking because they could talk, they had implants, and so the first couple hours, I was sitting there and there was no one else that could talk but me and everyone was doing sign and I'm like, oh God. (laughs) Like I was worried, and then –

INTERVIEWER: Can you understand sign?

ETHAN: I mean, at first at camp, I did not understand anything because we did do lessons in third and fourth grade for me, we had family lessons.

PAM: ... we had family lessons and they went to sign language camp.

ETHAN: And we learned a lot but we forgot it all because we didn't use it. And so I didn't remember anything except partially the alphabet ... But throughout the camp, I was really ... interested in learning ASL and – by the end of camp, I was able to have conversations with them.

PAM: And what did you tell me when you came home about being with people like you?

ETHAN: I've never really met anybody else who grew up deaf like me 'cause I've always been mainstreamed and so I've never met anybody who was deaf and was able to talk ... I've also met, you know, sixty-year-olds, forty-year-olds, fifty-year-olds that either were born deaf or lost their hearing midway through life and so they had implants, but ... as you get older, the brain elasticity, it gets worse, so they had struggles with the implants, which is understandable. But I've never (met) someone who got an implant at a young age so that they were able to be like me and there were like forty or fifty kids there that were like that, and so it was really – it was just an indescribable experience. It's just like, holy crap, there are people like this, like I didn't know that.

PAM: Which feels like a failing because we did all these events when they were young and a lot of places don't have them anymore.

ETHAN: They did try but there was just no one.

PAM: ... so it was just wonderful for him ...

ETHAN: They were from all over the country, California –

PAM: (overlapping) and he never had to explain himself to anybody. They knew, they knew what he was feeling. So it was just, we were very happy for him.

ETHAN: And also, like all of them were, they were deaf but ... they weren't Usher Syndrome, but my counselor, she did have Usher Syndrome and that was really cool.

I noticed on a chalk board in their kitchen a list of Spanish verbs and their conjugations. This prompted me to ask what languages they speak in their home.

They explained that they currently just speak English but Ethan and Gavin are making a commitment to learning Spanish.

Pam explained that, as with ASL, they had also been previously cautioned about using more than one language in the home, but "now we know we could have done Spanish from birth." Both Ethan and Gavin have made the decision to take Spanish in school instead of French, and other plans they have to learn the language together include making Spanish the language of their dinner conversations and going to the Dominican Republic for a month to stay with family and practice Spanish.

"And it's just brought us all up to another level."

When asked what was going well for their family, the Morrobels had a lot to say! Ethan explained that because balance difficulties are part of their Usher Syndrome, it's important for them to "keep a good core" and added, "Our athleticism is really, really good right now." They went on to explain that their move to New Jersey from Toronto contributed to their greater access to swim teams. One of the factors that supported this was that a waterproof case for their cochlear implant processors had been developed and, as Pam explained, "it has just been miraculous." Ethan had made the YMCA swim team three years ago and Gavin had made it two years ago.

Pam explained how, as a family, they've made deliberate choices to integrate activities that enhanced Ethan and Gavin's physical and language therapies into their daily routines in fun, engaging ways that brought them all together:

> we knew they didn't have balance, but no one seemed to be listening to us, so we would take them to specialist after specialist after specialist until we'd find somebody who knew what we were talking about ... we'd taken them to many physical therapists and occupational therapists who were great, but they still weren't getting what we were talking about.
>
> And we finally found a neuro physiotherapist and she's the one who got them on training to develop their cores and rather than a lot of exercises in a room, she started to take them outside, and she did it all ... like a physical trainer rather than a physical therapist. That's when they started to make it a lifelong activity ... it has to be how you live.

She went on to say more about the things they did when the children were younger,

> So, like we had a two-year old who was deaf here the other day and I was walking down the stairs with him and I was walking down like, 'Okay, here we go, down, Down, DOWN!' ... and that's what we did all the time ... we did that

and how they adapted family games as their needs changed:

... but then when they needed to develop their vocabulary more ... we started to do word games and bananagrams and that would be our family dinner game. And as they got older and needed to develop their general knowledge, that's when we started doing the trivia-like games that we did. So you know, it all evolved over time and we've just never stopped.

As the conversation about sports continued, Carlito attempted to list all the sports they were involved in and everyone had to join in to complete the tally that included surfing, swimming, tennis, racquetball, golf, baseball, soccer, basketball, volleyball, and skiing. He added that he thinks sports have helped teach Ethan and Gavin to never give up and that it "opens up ... a lot of doors because you meet people in all different walks."

Pam and Ethan shared additional insights on their family's joyful commitment to sports:

PAM: ... and we don't just do the sports we're comfortable in. You know, he coaches in baseball, I coach them both in basketball ... I asked Gavin, "Do you want me to coach again?" He said yes.

ETHAN: It's almost a joke now with my friends. Like every time they mention a sport, I'm like, 'Oh! I used to play it on a team in Canada.' And they're like, 'Oh my God!' It's like (laughs) they always ... name a random sport, like you know, one of those crazy ones, and they're like, 'Were you on a team like this in Canada?' (laughs)

Gavin described another activity that he and Ethan participate in and his reflection demonstrated his tenacity and his ability to pinpoint his own learning:

... we do this thing called Civil Air Patrol and it's basically the Air Forces Auxiliary, so like we do a lot of stuff there ... but I kind of lost interest since I got older, but I said I would give it a try, and I've almost done it two years now ... I've learned a lot in leadership and all that, so that's helped.

Ethan and Gavin have also invested in developing leadership skills through their involvement in the Leadership Training Conference. They were both nominated by their teachers to participate first as campers and then as junior counselors.

Ethan also identified "friends" as something else that was "going well." He admitted that before their last move to New Jersey, he was worried about making friends and how classmates may respond to his "ears" (throughout the interview, the Morrobels used this word to refer to Ethan and Gavin's cochlear implants):

how were they gonna react to my ears and whatever, 'cause I was going to be in seventh grade, so ... you know—the hormones are starting to kick in – but I made some key core friends ... for high school, you know, (snaps fingers) it really hardened the friendships … they sometimes forget that I'm deaf and then they're like, oh my God, you're deaf! (laughs) Like I go, what? And they're like, oh my God, I forgot you're deaf. And it's like, you know, that kind of thing. They always play, make jokes … It's like, you know, it's all fun and jokes. I think that's going really strong for me right now, just the support …

Gavin and Ethan identified some of their family's major strengths.

GAVIN: Our ability to work together … as my Mom and Dad were talking about before, how … my Mom's able to do the education part and all that, while my Dad's like researching and all that … If they weren't able to work together like that, I don't think we'd be nearly as successful as we are right now. And it's just brought us all up to another level … like we can work so efficiently without struggling … We all know what to do now. So that's helpful.

ETHAN: … We're a very outgoing family and that's been very helpful for us … I mean, for example … just being able to accommodate for ourselves … Like me and Gavin have learned that in the classroom sometimes our Mom's not always gonna be there, so we have to speak up for ourselves.

In the following exchange, the four of them talked more about the ways Ethan and Gavin are taking on additional personal responsibility:

PAM: … we like to do things together, and that's what we've always done. Even though it sometimes starts a little rough (laughs) and it's hard to get out the door, once we get there, we usually have a good time.

CARLITO: … sometimes we take it for granted … the checklist or the amount of things that we gotta worry about to get out the door.

ETHAN: Sleepovers for me are horrendous. Like my friends … they have their phone in their pocket and then that's it, they go and sleep over … I gotta come home, I gotta grab this big school backpack, chargers, batteries, like everything … My pockets are filled when we leave the house with all the stuff I need. And then we lose it sometimes, and we go ballistic.

CARLITO: It can get pricey. (laughs) That's a problem. It's pricey when we lose stuff.

PAM: I get upset when I told you exactly what you should do to avoid things like that and you don't do them.

GAVIN: We're only kids.

PAM: I know.

CARLITO: … We always struggle with the balance because they have a lot more responsibilities than other kids.

"The gem that they are."

When asked what they would like people to understand about Ethan and Gavin, Pam identified "their perseverance ... just never, never giving up, you know?" Ethan followed this up with examples from his experiences trying out for different sports teams and not being discouraged. Gavin brought up the idea that sometimes their competence can act as a liability as people around them can forget they have different needs:

> ... this can get annoying, what I want other people to know about me, specifically is that sometimes people forget that I have a disability and that sometimes I need stuff. So sometimes when I get extra time on a test or something like that, other kids are coming to tell me like, "Why do you need this? You can do everything else practically fine." And then sometimes it's hard to say to them I get tired easier ... this is what I need ... it's kind of like ... they get too used to me being able to do a lot of stuff I do that they forget that when I do need things, I need them ...

Ethan added his own examples:

ETHAN: I tell my friends all the time "...it's three times harder for me to walk than you. That's why I sweat so much." (laughs) And they're just like, "No, that's not possible." I'm like, "I'm telling you, it is harder for me to walk because I have no balance ... so I have to work harder to walk and that's why I sweat so much." 'Cause ... in gym, they're like, "Oh my God, you're sweating so much!" I'm like, "'Cause I'm working three times harder than you. That's how much better I am than you!"(laughs)

Pam added that it's not just peers that can lose sight of their need for accommodations:

> And then of course ... teachers too and that's when I step in for him. In high school there was one teacher who ... gave them a small card like this to be like a cheat sheet and you could write as much stuff on it as you wanted. And ... she wouldn't let Ethan have a bigger paper. So ... Ethan decided what he wanted and I wrote it all on this small little four-by-six card, and then I wrote it all on a five-by-seven card, and then I wrote it all on an eight-by-ten piece of paper. And I said, 'it's the same information but he needs this for his vision.' And she understood it at that point. And it's just, it's a lot of work, you know? And it's exhausting sometimes, most people don't understand how much work for them, for us, for the whole family it is every day, and like there's never a break.

They continued to talk more about some teachers' resistance to providing them with the necessary accommodations:

PAM: (She)didn't want to give the accommodations that he needed … she didn't understand why he needed them and wasn't really helpful

CARLITO: I don't know to what extent the success (pause) then overshadows their needs. Because they still don't portray the picture.

PAM: (overlapping) Yeah, it's why their diagnosis was late … Because they didn't look that they had no balance, but we were like, something's wrong. If you're not going to give us a diagnosis, we're gonna go get private physical therapy and help them, 'cause we know something's wrong with their balance … Teachers can't understand that you're not trying to make them have As … they have proven that they are A students.

CARLITO: … if you live it, so if you spend twenty-four hours with us or a couple of days then you start seeing the little things and say, Oh! … you don't wanna explain, you don't wanna take time … because it's not … to limit them. It's just, you know, this is who they are.

Carlito and Pam had a lot to say when considering the things they feel good about as parents:

PAM: (sighs) (pause) Gosh, if only we could have known this, you know, way back when … not everyone's made for university, but just to see what they're interested in … career paths are beyond what I ever imagined, so I'm just so proud of them and amazed by them … Everything's a bonus. Everything they do is a bonus 'cause we didn't expect it … And we've always had high expectations of them, but I've never worried about failure, but when they do succeed at things, it's not a surprise, but it's kind of like … I'm watching my … deaf-blind kid be a pitcher for the freshman baseball team.

Carlito joined in to explain how it can be challenging for him to keep from gushing about his boys:

CARLITO: Because, right, you don't want to be the guy that's always talking about yourself or your family –

ETHAN: But it's hard not to.

PAM: Right! (laughs)

CARLITO: … It's just like you wanna (pause) I know everybody probably feels like that about their own kids and their own families or whatever, but I feel like I always wanna just, I wanna share them. I wanna shout it out and … the gem that they are. (laughs)

INTERVIEWER: It's beautiful, it's a beautiful word.

ETHAN: Yeah. It's just, I think, what you're trying to say is we've all worked so hard—

CARLITO: Correct … And then it's almost like you wanna, you wanna share it, you wanna say something.

PAM: You want people to know that this just doesn't come from just getting a cochlear implant … or a diagnosis.

CARLITO: Exactly, to debunk a lot of it from the cochlear implant to the blindness to all of that because (pause) yeah, it's just, it's just hard work.

Ethan and Gavin are starting think about their futures and set goals:

ETHAN: I think just the general goal is graduate from college, get a good job … Engineering, more specifically, aerospace engineering 'cause I've always been interested in planes, rockets, outer space … And so you know, graduate from college, get a good job, and … if I had to say what my absolute dream job would be, it would be a worldwide photographer 'cause I love photography … landscapes and specifically sunrises and sunsets. My die-for pictures are sunrises and sunsets.

GAVIN: Me, like the same thing. Graduate from college, get a good job, start a family … kind of like aerospace engineer, but then … I also like the economics … thing.

CARLITO: Finance. He likes economics and finance …

GAVIN: Something like that, but getting a good job and have a good life, start a family, you know what I mean? I guess typical stuff. (laughs)

"But I don't care."

When the conversation moved to advice they've been given that they've found particularly helpful, Ethan emerged as the family philosopher. He started off by explaining a message that he took away from a retreat he had attended. "You're Amazing" not only expresses his own self-confidence and motivation, but also his appreciation for those around him. A distinctly positive, forward-moving thread ran through his personal mottos:

'Do what you can't.' That one's my own one … and that goes hand in hand with, 'You're not wasting time if you're enjoying it.'

He added:

'Make It Count,' 'Take One Step,' 'Don't Let Anyone Stop You,' 'Never Stop Trying,' 'Pave Your Path.'

CARLITO: All of those I think go right along with what we … said before that they never give up … it's all been about that. It's just try and try and keep going … I think that's what you guys have proven, right?

PAM: … it's funny because he took a motto like early on … He had to do a poem and 'But I Don't Care,' that was one of his mottos.

INTERVIEWER: So what does that mean, 'But I Don't Care'?

ETHAN: I always tell Gavin you gotta care less sometimes. You just, you gotta be the bigger man and let it go.

Pam read Ethan's poem aloud:

> Life has given me a lot of challenges, some I was too young to remember, but I don't care. I've always needed to use an FM system since I can remember. My eyes started to affect the way I worked in school when I was in grade four. I have a lot of things that make me different, but I don't care. I've always been thought of differently than normal people, but I don't care. I have a lot of challenges that I will face in the future, but I don't care. I choose to live my life the way I want it to be. I will always work hard and do the things that I want to do. The only thing that will ever really stop me is my disability but those are for reasonable reasons (laughs) like safety, but I don't care. I will find other things to do.

ETHAN: I don't care and never give up, those are my two big ones, I guess.

PAM: Yeah, they're consistent.

INTERVIEWER: Can you think of situations that have kind of brought you back to those two?

ETHAN: Never give up. I always remember baseball before we moved here, I never made the rep team which was the travel team, and then I came here, I tried out, and I kept trying out and I made the travel team here … And the, 'But I don't care' is my brother here, he always complains how people are asking over and over and over again why do you need this, why do you need that? I tell him this is it, this is why you need it, and if they come again, then I'll tell them again, I don't care.

GAVIN: I'll tell them again, it's just it's annoying … Like let's say first of all, I can't see very well at night and stuff like that, and I tell most of them that, and then … I'd say, 'Oh yeah, I can't see,' and then they keep on asking why, and then I'm just like, every time I go out at night, it's so annoying having to tell every single person you've already told them like five times already.

Gavin shared the words that he finds inspirational:

> 'Never Give Up.' I mean, that's one, and then also, 'You Can Do It.' … I always think about that one before like, let's say, a swimming race or stuff like that … in my head I'm saying, 'You can do it, just try your hardest.'

Carlito and Pam shared some of their own maxims:

CARLITO: I guess I am naïve about people. I like to see the good side of everything, so I'm a very happy-go-lucky kind of guy, and I think that has helped
me approach our family situation from Day One. So glass half full instead of
half empty, and all the ones that go with that. And another one, I have a
little banner in the office, and it's in Spanish. Basically, 'you cannot get to
the sunrise unless you go through the path of night.' In Spanish it's very
poetic in the way that the words rhyme and all that, and it has a little
mountain and a little river … if you do go through the process, the light, the
sunrise, it will be there and, so I think we've gone through a little process
and you guys are sun – the sun is about to come out.

PAM: Many years ago … I took a quote from a book, it was written within the
text, and it was in teaching. It was 'Fair Is Not Equal.' … I have it on my
business cards, I have it on the wall of my office, and I think it just applies
for everything.

CARLITO: There is the 'You Gotta Earn It.'

INTERVIEWER: Is that something that you hear Pam say a lot?

CARLITO: Well, she's very driven. And it's not like by chance. You get what you
put in.

"it's not what you think they need, it's what they know they need."

When asked what advice they would offer other families, Gavin started the conversation with, "Work hard." Carlito contributed, "Advocate" and Ethan added,
"Embrace." Pam discussed some of her own advocacy efforts and strategies:

I recently wrote to the mayor to ask him to recognize Usher Syndrome
Awareness Day, so there's many things I do on my own, but I always include
them, so they came with us and they accepted it and … spoke out. So just,
it's their disability and they need to be involved, aware, and comfortable
from a very young age.

When talking about dealing with the boys' schools, she pointed out the reciprocal nature of accommodations:

we try to be accommodating for the school 'cause we know it's not easy for
them—to meet the needs for every student, but also what they need is
important, so I'm always trying to be accommodating as well … But you
can't be in there demanding all the time … they'll usually work with us if
we're willing to work with them …

Pam captured her advice to other families in her "Top Ten Tips for Parents" that she published as part of the Sound Intuition blog that she contributes to; it is shared at the end of this chapter. Many of these suggestions are brought to life in the stories and experiences the Morrobels shared.

They also had advice to share with professionals. Pam started off by explaining the importance of reaching out in ways that build partnerships with whole families, stressing valuing the role of fathers:

> we went through a lot of things as a family, therapy sessions, whatever, events, we always went together as a family, and he would try to make as many appointments as he could … he still does … everybody embraces it … And for a therapist, that would be the advice, encourage Dads to come. And just make it not just about therapy … It's not one size fits all, so each disability, each family, or each kid, it's individual, so it's just about having that patience and open-mindedness to it, right? Especially in some of the cases that do not (pause) paint the picture, or disability is not obvious.

Gavin had different advice to offer professionals. His powerful suggestions were rooted in his experiences.

> GAVIN: … I feel like professionals, like especially teachers, should know that it's not what you think they need, it's what they know they need … the reason why I say that is because I had one experience with that in like a teacher really didn't want to give me what I needed … She kind of just like (pause) gave me … what she thought I needed and then stuck with that instead of listening to us.

Ethan offered an example of how simple and powerful it can be for teachers to take the opposite approach:

> For example, today, my chem teacher, he said, "Ethan, could you stay after class?" I did. And he was like, "Hey, what do I need to do to help you?" And (snaps fingers) that's it. That's all you need to do … That's what you want to hear.

"but it may also be the best thing that will ever happen to you."

Gavin had a profound insight into how his and Ethan's Usher Syndrome has strengthened their family's connection:

> … from most of the people that I hear that have had Usher's Syndrome for like a decent amount … for like most of our childhood or let's say they're adults … it may be the worst thing that's ever happened to you, but it may also be the best thing that will ever happen to you … It's that like even

though, yes, it's so painful to hear that either your son has it or that you yourself has it as an adult ... Yes, it may (pause) stop you from doing some stuff, but it provides so much more (pause) I don't know how to say it, but I don't think our family would have been as connected ... if we didn't have this. So, it's like a benefit that we can talk to each other, and some other families can't really talk to each other as well as we can, and it's like a good thing that we can just all embrace it ...

At the end of our second interview, Pam and Carlito reflected on the experience:

CARLITO: It's been quite the journey.

PAM: Yeah, we've thoroughly enjoyed doing this.

CARLITO: This part, yes, it just kind of brings back and we kind of forget about all the things—

PAM: It has been very nice, though, to reflect back and (pause) see all the things that we've done.

INTERVIEWER: Is there anything you want to say to each other as we finish up?

CARLITO: Love you all.

INTERVIEWER: Remember when he called them "gems"?

PAM: Yes.

INTERVIEWER: That was lovely.

PAM: Wonderful family bringing-together-moment for us, I think. 'Cause as they're getting older, we're separating, even though we still do the Family Dinner Game. But – I just always say we listen to everything every doctor ever said to us ... and it's not easy to do, but I think (pause) involving everybody has been the key for our family.

Pam shared the following strategies for parents on the Sound Intuition blog.

My Top Ten Tips for Parents:

1. *Determine desired outcomes* for your child and choose the intervention approach and professionals who will help your family achieve them.
2. *Clearly state the family's goals and expectations* to every professional involved, so everyone is on the same page. At the same time, be open to new ideas.
3. *When visiting a clinic, walk its halls*, saying hi to everyone on each visit, not just the professional being seen that day.
4. *Turn appointments into an adventure* and plan something fun to do that day after the appointment, especially if you are traveling. If an appointment that is close by, get a special treat afterwards.
5. *Give respect if you want respect back.* Be timely and polite, not demanding. Also, be personal and ask about family. Encourage your child to do the same.

6. *Inform professionals of the extra-curricular activities in which your child is involved* enabling them to develop an intervention plan that can be incorporated into those sports/activities. Professionals may also choose to use extra-curricular themes in their therapy plans.

7. *Include and involve school professionals* in the intervention process by sharing goals and expectations.

8. *Share important events/successes/accomplishments* with each member of the intervention team, helping the professionals get to know your child.

9. *Help your child develop self-advocacy skills* by having professionals direct questions to the child from an early age. Make the children the focal point of appointments – after all, he/she know themselves best. Also involve your child in his/her 'Identification, Placement & Review Committee' (IPRC) meetings. This will help your child gain confidence and greater understanding of his/her strengths and needs.

10. *Become involved* in professional training, advocacy and fundraising organizations focused on your child's needs. This will further develop the child's and family's self-advocacy skills.

> P. Aasen (2016, July 28). The "poetry" of parent-professional partnership
> [Blog post]. Retrieved from/http://soundintuition.com/blog/pam-aasen-the-
> poetry-of-professional-partnerships)

Questions for Discussion

1. How would you describe the Morrobel family's strengths and resources?

2. This family demonstrates a strong commitment to teamwork. Pam and Carlito are deliberate in the ways they foster their sons' self-confidence and ability to advocate for themselves from a very early age. As a professional, how can you support families to develop these capacities and perspectives?

3. The Morrobel family experienced a model of family-centered practice during their time at "Sick Kids Hospital" in Toronto. They continue to approach relationships with professionals in a very thoughtful way. What are some of the strategies that they bring to developing these partnerships? As a professional, how can you help nurture strong, reciprocal partnerships with families?

8

AN UNEXPECTED RECIPROCITY: GUEST SPEAKERS LEARN BY SHARING THEIR STORIES

In each of the previous chapters, families share their stories and experiences as a way to offer professionals and teachers-in-training new insights and understanding. This chapter describes how families, individuals with disabilities, and professionals in related fields, were integrated into a graduate course on working with families of children with disabilities as guest speakers. As expected, the students' learning was enhanced as the speakers' personal stories brought the course topics to life. Through class discussions and assignments, students shared thoughtful insights and connections between guest speakers' experiences and course content.

However, by taking the next step of listening to the guest speakers not only during their class presentations but also in individual interviews, it was revealed that sharing their stories yielded a surprising outcome for them as well. They described the experience as an "honor," "privilege," and "very, very important" and they recognized its power to help them "be reflective," "share what I know," and make them "not to be sad." This project was designed to learn more about why these individuals agreed to speak to future teachers and what they gained from the experience of sharing their stories. The participants' responses to the interview questions illuminate that the act of telling their stories was transformative for the storytellers, as well as for the story listeners, and served, in part, as the inspiration for this book.

Background

Including professionals from across disciplines in teacher education exposes students to a range of career possibilities and simultaneously makes them aware of the various supports available to children and families, laying the groundwork for professional collaboration (Goldfarb et al., 2010; Prater, Sileo, & Black, 2000).

Similarly, integrating family members into teacher education and training has been identified as a way to model building partnerships with families and enacting family-centered practice (Knapp-Philo, Corso, Brekken, & Heal, 2004; Murray, Curran, & Zellers, 2008; Prosser, 2009).

Previous studies have suggested that the use of course guest speakers can offer students opportunities to enrich their understanding of content and begin to develop the necessary skills and dispositions that foster professionals' capacity for strong, reciprocal partnerships with families (Blue-Banning, Summers, Frankland, Nelson, & Beegle, 2004; Knapp-Philo, Corso, Brekken, & Heal, 2004; Murray, Curran & Zellers, 2008; Prosser, 2009). Guest speakers sharing their family stories have been especially useful at reaching those who demonstrate resistance to certain values and outlooks (Kubal, Meyler, Stone, & Mauney, 2003). A parent who participated in co-instruction of pre-service early childhood special educators explained it this way, "The university class is a prime opportunity to educate and sensitize students to families' needs, concerns, and knowledge" (McBride, Sharp, Hains, & Whitehead, 1995, p. 344).

The family-centered model is an enactment of a strengths-based empowerment approach that has been shown to yield better outcomes for individuals and families (Bailey, 2001; Barrera & Corso, 2002; Coots, 2007; Harry, 1997; Turnbull, Turnbull, Erwin, Soodak, & Shogren, 2014.) The fields of healthcare, social work, and education are all moving away from a traditional medical model towards a relationship-based approach that recognizes families as resources (Goldfarb et al., 2010; Murray, Ackerman-Spain, Williams, & Ryley, 2011). By including families as guest speakers in the course, I modeled the importance of listening to families and accessing their unique stories and insights. Not only were families and our partnerships with them positioned as resources, but each family's unique constellation of strengths were brought to light and celebrated. During these class visits, students were given the opportunity to practice listening to families and engaging in conversations with them in a safe, supportive environment.

People with disabilities have also been integrated into teacher preparation coursework. Jorgenson and colleagues (Jorgensen, Bates, Frechette, Sonnenmeier, & Curtin, 2011) explain that, at the University of New Hampshire, three courses are collaboratively taught by faculty and individuals with disabilities. They describe how this model enacts the "Nothing About Us Without Us" maxim that dictates that "any activity that *affects* people with disabilities – legislation, policy, research, professional preparation, disability services, etc. – should *involve* people with disabilities in leadership roles" (p. 11). One co-instructor, a woman with Asperger's Syndrome, explained it this way:

> I feel that by offering my viewpoint to the scholars, it will help them to better appreciate what it's like to live with an ASD every day. I want to better equip professionals and upcoming professionals in the field of ASD with an understanding of how ASD makes us think or act differently and

what they can do to help us achieve to our fullest potential and beyond … I wanted the scholars to learn from me … (that) we are all individuals, who happen to have very diverse abilities, dreams, need and wants (Jorgensen et al., 2011, pp. 115–118.)

Listening to Guest Speakers inside and outside of the College Classroom

As the course instructor for a Masters level education course on Partnerships with Families of Children with Disabilities, I invited a range of guest speakers to come and share their experiences in order to offer my students direct access to individuals with disabilities and their families as well as to professionals in the field. I drew on both professional and personal relationships to recruit colleagues, family members of children with disabilities, and adults with disabilities working as Self Advocates for the State Self Advocacy Association.

Through informal conversations with several of these individuals over the subsequent semesters, I came to understand that, in addition to my students gaining from this experience, the guest speakers themselves were also identifying benefits to their participation. To get a clearer sense of the ways connecting with pre-service teachers and sharing their stories was impacting them I decided to interview the guest speakers over the next academic year to learn what motivated them to agree to participate in the class sessions and what they gained from the experience.

With the exception of Linda's interview, which took place in her home the week following her most recent visit to my class, the one-on-one interviews were conducted in my office directly after the course session the speaker had attended. Since several of the guest speakers had already participated in the course multiple times by the semester the project was conducted, their responses often reflected their cumulative experience and insights.

I used a brief protocol of prepared questions to guide the interviews; however, they were conducted in a flexible and responsive way "because as qualitative researchers we are constantly evolving instruments and because settings and people are also dynamic and diverse" (Brantlinger, Jimenez, Klinger, Pugach, & Richardson, 2005, p. 197). I invited participants to share their ideas and stories using open-ended questions and seizing opportunities to turn interviews into conversations while being careful not to lead their responses. The interviews were recorded and transcribed and I read through the transcripts several times to become familiar with each speaker's stories and perspectives. Using the project questions as a frame, I searched for points of overlap and divergence.

The following is a summary of the guest speakers who were participants in this project:

Todd	Father of a young son with Asperger's Syndrome
Linda	Mother of a deceased daughter with a seizure disorder
Carmen	Mother of an adult son who is deaf and blind Families Specialist working with families with children who are deaf and blind
Nettie	Adult with a disability working as Self Advocate for the State Self Advocacy Association
Andrea	Regional Coordinator of State Self Advocacy Association
Katie	Director of NICU Family Center Developmental Care
Leslie	Founding Director of Early Intervention agency

Insights Shared

When asked why they agreed to be guest speakers and what they gained from the experience, participants' responses reflected the following themes:

1. Personal Favor to Personal and Professional Growth
2. Teachers Positioned to Make a Difference
3. The Power of Sharing Your Story.

Personal Favor to Personal and Professional Growth

Several of the participants shared that while they initially agreed to be a guest speaker as a personal favor, the experience led to personal and/or professional growth and commitment. Todd, a father of a young son with Asperger's Syndrome who attended the university-based childcare center where the course was offered, explained how a personal favor turned into a commitment to advocacy in this way:

> ... it was always in the back of my mind, there's a very strong advocacy group, you know or advocacy side to parents of autistic children ... Both my wife and I work full time ... devoting all my time to helping my son, there's just no way that I could give any time to those groups that are just doing such amazing work. So, when Lena (the center director) originally mentioned it to me ... my first response was 'Sure, you know, Lena, if you want me to do something I'll do it. You know, you've been so great to us, why wouldn't I do it right?' But as I thought about it more I really saw it as my little bit of advocacy not just for my son, but for autism as a whole ... So, I mean it became for me ... why I put the time into it and prepared for it was because I view it as very, very important.

Like Todd, Leslie also had a connection and commitment to the university. As my former graduate student, our continued personal and professional relationship influenced her decision to return as a guest speaker. Leslie is the founding director of an Early Intervention agency that specializes in supporting families that have participated in international adoptions.

She explained how her personal connection to the college and to me initially inspired her to agree to be a guest speaker. Also, while she started off wanting to contribute to other students' growth, she realized that the experience also allowed her to recognize her own accomplishments:

> I do it for myself, you know, to keep in touch with the institution and make connections and network and I truly enjoy it. Most importantly I have a personal connection to my professor and that keeps me coming back to the college and to wherever she may travel. I look forward to this and it is truly a pleasure ... It's an honor to be asked, and I feel good doing it. It forces me to be reflective and it's a really nice method for me to see personally, how far I've come as a professional, and how far my agency has come ... I remember not so long ago sitting on the other side of the table, and being a student and having guest speakers come in, and being inspired.

Linda was the mother of a child, Lucy, that I had worked with through home-based Early Intervention several years earlier. As we sat together in her home conducting the interview, she shared a little bit about her family's story:

> At the age of five and a half months, Lucy became severely sick, with a condition called myoclonic seizures, and it was pretty hard to know that your firstborn has some you know, disabilities ... But life has, it hasn't been easy ... maybe my Lord gave me the strength to be able to move on and just see Lucy as a person, not as a job.

Linda explained that, initially, she agreed to speak in the class because she wanted to do something nice for me by helping me with the upcoming course I'd be teaching. But a few months later, before the start of the semester when I'd be teaching the course, Lucy died at the age of 6. Linda shared how Lucy's death reinforced her decision to address the class:

> Well, you know, because, it made me feel good ... during that time, I was really, really sad, but everywhere I went, I talked about her. So that made me not to be sad. Every time I left there, I said, 'We did it again, Lucy. We helped another child' ... Every time I would say, 'High five – we did it again. You were my voice this time. You talked through me.'

In reaching out to help other children, Linda was also finding a way to carry Lucy with her.

Todd, Leslie, and Linda all consented to joining the course as guest speakers as a personal favor and a way to support children, families and prospective teachers. Through the experience, they also each gained insight into their own personal and professional growth.

Teachers Positioned to Make a Difference

Nearly all of the participants commented that one of the main reasons why they agreed to be guest speakers for this class of future teachers was their recognition of the important role that teachers play in the lives of children with disabilities and their families. Below are a few examples.

Katie was the director of Family Center Developmental Care at an urban hospital that supports infants in the Neonatal Intensive Care Unit (NICU) and their families during their very first days and throughout their time in Early Intervention. Katie had previously taught this course and, at the time of the interview, was returning as a guest speaker for the third time. She explained her commitment as a guest speaker in this way:

> Well, what makes me continue to come back is that I know that there's always a new group of students who have never been exposed to the NICU ... So every time you have a new group of students there's a new opportunity.

Linda shared her own feelings about how teachers, specifically those working with very young children with disabilities and their families in their homes, are positioned to offer children and families a range of support:

> You come into a house where this child, this family needs help, you could be like the person to help them. Help them get all the services they need. Even if that's the only thing you do for them. But at least help them get the services that they need.

With pride, she explained that now Lucy had a role in preparing teachers, "When I spoke to them tonight Lucy was teaching teachers."

Carmen, the mother of an adult son who is deaf and blind, who also works as a Families Specialist working with families with children who are deaf and blind, had been a guest speaker in the course several times. She explained what kept her returning:

> I love talking to teachers and thank you for allowing me to do that. My son was born and I did not have any support while Keith was zero to three. And one of the dreams in my life was to help families who have newborn babies because I think that if somebody would've gotten a hold of me when Keith was two, three months old my entire life, Keith's whole entire life, would've

been very different ... And now I do have an opportunity to talk to ... to allow young teachers who are working with young kids to understand how we parents feel. I think that's really my privilege and something I really wanted to do my whole entire life ... It's really a privilege. I think it's really wonderful to see the young teachers, young faces coming into the field.

Carmen discussed evolutions in the field that have contributed to relationships between professionals and families developing into true partnerships:

CARMEN: New teachers coming into the field are pioneers ... they're coming into the field with a new mentality. They're coming in thinking that parents are equal to them, which is not the same thing we had twenty years ago when I really started fighting to obtain Keith's services.

INTERVIEWER: What do you attribute that change to?

CARMEN: A very, very serious movement on the parent networks and parents' associations which one day woke up and said, 'You know, enough is enough and we don't want to be discriminated against' ... They know their rights. And therefore, they can talk to a teacher on an equal-to-equal basis ... So, you as a teacher, have to respond saying, 'you know what, I'd better work with this family because they know what they want and if I can partner with them, we are going to obtain better results for the children' ... the new teachers that we are seeing coming into the field, they know how to negotiate situations with the families, and that's wonderful!

Todd expressed a similar sentiment about the opportunity to speak about autism to students preparing to be teachers. He recognized the exponential impact he could have by speaking to a group of prospective teachers.

I mean this epidemic is touching you know, one out of every one hundred and fifty kids ... More and more of these kids are going to be in mainstream and so every educator has to know this stuff and I really feel like it's actually a great thing for me to be able to talk to so many of them and share what I know.

Nettie, the Self Advocate, also made a connection between the influence of teachers and her interest in being a guest speaker for the course. Like Carmen, she drew on her own previous experiences with professionals and recognized their evolving roles.

This generation of teachers is more interested in looking at the human being as the person in the inside of the heart ... They want to study and they are more prepared. So, I think for us, that's absolutely wonderful to see them more prepared and interested in asking us questions.

She went on to explain the expanded role that she felt teachers should take on:

We need our teachers to be our friends, you know, our pals sometimes …
someone who is teaching in the class, but who says, 'are you ok?' A friend …
that will be a role model; you might not know what that role model might
mean to them and how far that role model would take them.

Parents, professionals, and individuals with disabilities all acknowledged the
powerful impact that teachers had on the lives of children with disabilities and
their families. They capitalized on the opportunity to speak to future educators
knowing that through them they could enact positive support and understanding
for other individuals and families. Guest speakers like Carmen and Nettie,
recognized that this new generation of teachers are approaching their work with
students and families with an openness of mind and heart. When families, individuals with disabilities, and professionals in related fields, are integrated into
teacher preparation, an expectation of partnership and collaboration is set.
Emerging professionals are given the message that they're entering a field that
values teamwork and collegiality. They're not expected to have all the answers,
but they are expected to work with students, families, and colleagues to discover
and create solutions together.

The Power of Sharing Your Story

Just as previous studies explained that the telling of one's story makes it salient
and that sharing family stories helps parents "reframe their family's situation"
(Kim & Vail, 2011, p. 352), several of the guest speakers talked about their belief
in the power of sharing their personal stories. Katie discussed the importance of
hearing the stories of families who have beginnings in the NICU, "Early childhood special ed students really need to know that these families have very different beginnings, that they have very real needs and that they should continue to
listen to their stories."

Andrea from the Self Advocacy Association explained her work in this way:

I'm the regional coordinator of the state Self Advocacy Association …
Basically our mission is that we are fighting for equality and rights for
people with developmental disabilities … I'm sort of a minority in my
organization. There are only a few supportive coordinating roles and then
the majority of people employed by Self Advocacy are people with
developmental disabilities … it really has been cool to play the role of
facilitator and just see how much the audiences can learn just from
hearing their first-hand experiences. And also, I myself, of course, learn
from the Self Advocates all the time.

She described the unique impact of hearing the Self Advocates share their personal stories:

> I think that when the audience hears from the Self Advocates themselves, they can't do that separating thing we do when we hear a professional talking ... When the audience is forced to hear it through the mouth of the person themselves who is living it, they're forced to kind of set aside their judgments and preconceived notions ... It kind of takes down that barrier that people, you know, subconsciously put up.

Linda described her feelings about sharing her story very simply and poignantly:

> It makes me feel good that Lucy was useful. You know. And she still is. And I always thought that maybe my story could help other people ... And it stopped me from thinking about that she was no longer here.

Linda's words convey her recognition that the process of sharing her story helped not only the listeners but also herself. In his story, *The Zahir*, Paulo Coelho (2005) describes the effect in this way, "... because when people tell their stories, they feel braver" (p. 182).

Dr. Jonathan Adler, the co-director of Health Story Collaborative and a professor of narrative, champions the use of story as a way to bring patients and providers together (Adler, 2012). He identifies agency and communion as two story elements that contribute to improved well-being. This chapter's guest speakers and the families in this book convey their stories in ways that help them feel in control of their lives and surrounded by supportive relationships. Sharing their narratives can help them make meaning of their experiences and can deepen and fortify their partnerships with professionals (Beck, 2015). As we listen to individuals with disabilities, their family members, and professionals in the field, we learn what they value about sharing their stories and participating in the preparation of teachers. Their stories both reflect their growth and development and contribute to ours.

References

Adler, J. M. (2012). Living into the story: Agency and coherence in a longitudinal study of narrative identity development and mental health over the course of psychotherapy. Paper 1.http://digitalcommons.olin.edu/facpub_2012/1

Bailey, D. B. J. (2001). Evaluating parent involvement and family support in early intervention and preschool programs. *Journal of Early Intervention*, 24, 1–14.

Barrera, I., & Corso, R. (2002). Cultural competency as skilled dialogue. *Topics in Early Childhood Special Education*, 22(2), 103–113.

Beck, C. (2015). Life stories. *The Atlantic Monthly*, August 10, 2015.

Blue-Banning, M., Summers, J. A., Frankland, H. C., Nelson, L. L., & Beegle, G. (2004). Dimensions of family and professional partnerships: Constructive guidelines for collaboration. *Exceptional Children*, 70(2), 167–184.

Brantlinger, E., Jimenez, R., Klinger, J., Pugach, M., & Richardson, V. (2005). Qualitative studies in special education. *Exceptional Children*, 71(2), 195–207.

Coelho, P. (2005). *The zahir*. New York: Harper Collins.

Coots, J. J. (2007). Building bridges with families: Honoring the mandates of IDEA. *Issues in Teacher Education*, 16(2), 33–40.

Goldfarb, F., Devine, K., Yingling, J., Hill, A., Moss, J., Ogburn, E., & Roberts, R. (2010). Partnering with professionals: Family-centered care from the parent perspective. *Journal of Family Social Work*, 13, 91–99.

Harry, B. (1997). Leaning forward or bending backwards: Cultural reciprocity in working with families. *Journal of Early Intervention*, 21(1), 62–72.

Jorgensen, C. M., Bates, K., Frechette, A. H., Sonnenmeier, R. M., & Curtin, J. (2011). "Nothing about us without us": Including people with disabilities as teaching partners in university courses. *International Journal of Whole Schooling*, 7(2), 109–126.

Kim, E. J., & Vail, C. (2011). Improving preservice teachers' perspectives on family involvement in teaching children with special needs: Guest speakers versus video. *Teacher Education and Special Education: The Journal of Teacher Education Division of the Council for Exceptional Children*, 34(4), 320–338.

Knapp-Philo, J., Corso, R. M., Brekken, L., & Heal, H. (2004). Training strategies for the 21st century. *Infants and Young Children*, 17(2), 171–183.

Kubal, T., Meyler, D., Stone, R. T., & Mauney, T. T. (2003). Teaching diversity and learning outcomes: Bringing lived experience into the classroom. *Teaching Sociology*, 31, 441–455.

McBride, S. L., Sharp, L., Hains, A. H., & Whitehead, A. (1995). Parents as co-instructors in preservice training: A pathway to family-centered practice. *Journal of Early Intervention*, 19(4), 343–389.

Murray, M. M., Ackerman-Spain, K., Williams, E. U., & Ryley, A. T. (2011). Knowledge is power: Empowering the autism community through parent-professional training. *The School Community Journal*, 21(1), 19–36.

Murray, M., Curran, E., & Zellers, D. (2008). Building parent/professional partnerships: An innovative approach for teacher education. *Teacher Educator*, 43(2), 87–108.

Prater, M. A., Sileo, T. W. & Black, R. S. (2000). Preparing educators and related school personnel to work with at-risk students, *Teacher Education and Special Education: The Journal of Teacher Education Division of the Council for Exceptional Children*, 23(1), 51–64.

Prosser, T. M. (2009). Personnel preparation for preservice early intervention providers: Supporting families' participation in university classrooms. *Journal of Early Childhood Teacher Education*, 30, 69–78.

Turnbull, A. P., Turnbull, H. R., Erwin, E., Soodak, L., & Shogren, K. (2014). *Families, professionals, and exceptionality: Positive outcomes through partnerships and trust* (7th ed.). Columbus: Pearson/Merrill Prentice Hall Publishing Company.

9

SUMMARY AND CONCLUDING THOUGHTS

The chapters in this book bring the voices of families of children with disabilities to the page, allowing readers access to the rich diversity of their thoughts, feelings, ideas, strategies, perspectives, challenges, and achievements. Each of the families represents a unique set of life circumstances; their children are in different stages of childhood, they negotiate a variety of special needs, and they are diverse in their cultures, their family structures, and their beliefs. Yet across these differences, their stories also echo shared experiences and feelings that, taken together, can greatly inform and expand our understanding about what it means to be a family that includes a child with special needs (Bayat, 2007; González, Moll, & Amanti, 2005).

The children represented in these chapters range from preschoolers to high schoolers. In one of the chapters they are actual participants in the conversation, while in others they come to life through the words of their mothers, fathers, and in one case, grandmother (Crettenden, Lam, & Denson, 2018; Lee & Gardner, 2010). Although the families all live within the same regional area in the United States, they represent a range across ethnicity, culture, and socioeconomic status. In three of the families, there are two siblings with disabilities, and in two of the families there are other siblings or half-siblings (Barr & McLeod, 2010). In some cases, extended family members are close by and in others they live in other states or countries. The nature of their family support systems varies widely, with some families finding the greatest support from professionals (Ludlow, Skelly, & Rohleder, 2012).

In this final chapter, we bring together the overarching themes that grow out of the chapter stories to provide an overview of what the families tell us. Using our interview protocol as a guide, and informed by all the conversations, we highlight those aspects of the stories that resonate across families in particular ways

(Goodley & Tregaskis, 2006; Maul & Singer, 2009; Slattery, McMahon, & Gallagher, 2017). As discussed in our introductory chapter, we continue to look through a lens of "goodness" (Lawrence-Lightfoot, 2016, p. 20) as we uncover the strengths and resources that families bring, as well as the choices they make in response to life challenges. We integrate and summarize their shared hopes, inspirations, and dreams for their children, and their advice for other parents and for professionals (Blue-Banning, Summers, Frankland, Nelson, & Beegle, 2004; Prezant & Marshak, 2006).

In reading the chapter stories, a powerful sense of love and commitment comes through in each of the families. They speak of the ways they work together as a team, advocate for their children, engage siblings in care and advocacy, and enjoy being together. Although they share many ongoing challenges, they demonstrate a great deal of resilience (Bayat, 2007) and optimism toward the future (Slattery et al., 2017). Similar to the families in Maul and Singer's (2009) study, they are resourceful in finding strategies and making accommodations that work for them as families that include children with disabilities.

In addition to the strength that comes through their family bonds, they are also resourceful in drawing on their own personal and professional strengths. Some of the parents have a background in education which provides a useful framework for accessing services for their children; one father, a parent of a child with many technology needs, has professional skills in technology; in one family, the grandmother, who is a primary caregiver for a child with medical needs, is a nurse. Many family members find strength in their spiritual beliefs, which help guide difficult decisions and offer support and hope. One mother attributes the inner strength that keeps her going to her own experience as a child refugee.

The families have also become quite adept at accessing outside resources to help their children. They skillfully navigate the bureaucracy of local and state support programs, investigate avenues for acquiring specialized equipment, and find home-based services to meet their children's needs. Many of the families spoke of the strength they've found in connecting with other families of children with disabilities (Ludlow et al., 2012). Some talked about the supportive role of extended family, especially grandmothers (Crettenden et al., 2018; Lee & Gardner, 2010; Puig, 2012) who offer love and encouragement that keeps them going, and sometimes direct care for their children. Families have also found strength in some of their relationships with professionals (Blue-Banning et al., 2004). One mother referred to these professional partners as "her warriors on the ground" and the "little angels" that pushed her along.

All of the families represented in these chapters poignantly expressed their wish that others would see their children as "human, like everybody else." We hear their pleas for recognition of their children's dignity in comments like "he has feelings like anyone else," "he has his own personality," "they're not sick," "you don't have to be sorry," and "advocate for him and his community – they are smart, aware, sensitive, but different." They would like others to truly value their children.

Families also expressed that they and their children are working hard to do all that they can to live full and rewarding lives. Sometimes their children do need something different that others might not need. They hoped that people would make responsive accommodations and be empathic without being overly sympathetic (Maul & Singer, 2009). One mother shared her wish that other parents would allow their children to respond naturally to her child, rather than imposing their own biases onto them (Farrugia, 2009). She hoped that other parents would set the tone for greater inclusion of children with disabilities at school and in the community.

Each of the families expressed their hope that others would see their children as unique and special people, with their own personalities, interests, sensitivities, and intelligences. Ultimately, they want others to treat their children with the same care and respect they would show toward anyone else.

In the story chapters, our conversations reveal ongoing challenges in everyday life that are echoed in research on families of children with disabilities. The impact of issues such as challenging behavior (Dunlap & Fox, 2007), other people's judgments, lack of support, social isolation (Ludlow et al., 2012), dealing with stigma (Farrugia, 2009), and the financial hardship and amount of work required to raise a child with a developmental disability (Maul & Singer, 2009) are discussed within different families. Many of the families shared their ongoing struggle with finding appropriate educational programs and supports for their children, which may involve battling with district personnel, or even hiring a lawyer to negotiate on their behalf. The costs of finding and paying for expert therapists and doctors, specialized equipment, or private educational programs can be prohibitive for some families.

Particularly for those families whose children may display unexpected social behaviors, other people's reactions in public places, and their ways of being insensitive and hurtful, can be an ongoing source of stress. These families shared that it can be difficult to talk to friends and family about their children's issues, which are sometimes perceived as the result of poor parenting. Values and expectations for children could be interpreted through different cultural lenses. This emerged, for example, during visits to home countries, in interactions with extended family, and in navigating community experiences. Children's behavior can also get in the way of meeting their educational needs. When professionals focus on managing challenging behavior at the expense of other areas of growth and development, children's right to developmentally appropriate teaching and learning is compromised.

Bias and stigma were revealed by one mother who gave birth to her child as a teenager. She talked about the way she was treated by a doctor who assumed that her baby would not live. Other mothers talked about being judged by professionals and struggling to hold on to their hopes for their child in the face of a deficit-oriented approach to assessment and intervention (Maul & Singer, 2009; Lee, Park, & Recchia, 2016). These early negative experiences with professionals can leave deep impressions on families, adding to their feelings of social isolation and coloring their notions about collaborating to meet their children's needs (Dunlap & Fox, 2007).

The families shared a variety of goals and dreams that they hold for their children, with an overwhelmingly positive emphasis on being happy (Slattery et al., 2017). Many talked about the possibility of their children going on to college, getting married if they chose to, and having a family. Some emphasized that they wanted their children to be productive and make a contribution to society, while others focused more on hoping they would have the opportunity to more fully develop their skills, talents, and abilities.

Almost all of the families talked about their hope that their children would be able to live independent lives, and to be able to advocate for themselves in some way, which was expressed by some as both a hope and a fear that it might not come to be (Ludlow et al., 2012). Some families talked about the possibility of assisted living arrangements for their children, and some families worried about the kind of care their children might receive when they could no longer care for them. One mother described her dream for her children's care as "What would I want my mother to do for me?" One father hoped for technological advances, such as stem cell and gene therapy, that would give his son with physical disabilities greater access to the world around him.

Overall, the families desired that their children would go on to have a good life, to be content with themselves, and to find social connections with others. Although they knew that future caregivers might not love them as their families did, their thoughts about their children's future were full of hope and possibility (Maul & Singer, 2009; Slattery et al., 2017).

As documented in the literature, families had a lot to say about their relationships with professionals (Dunlap & Fox, 2007; Goodley & Tregaskis, 2006). For many of the families, these interactions began very early in their children's lives and for most will continue far into the future. Some families had very powerful memories of negative experiences with professionals, such as the doctor who told one teenage mother she did not plan to monitor her baby after birth, given the severity of his prenatal diagnosis; another mother felt that the early intervention system took away her self-efficacy as a parent. Other families reported interactions with doctors and other professionals that were not helpful, and that left them feeling discouraged and uncertain about their children's future.

Over time, many of the families were able to forge positive working relationships with a wide variety of service providers, medical assistants, and therapists. They came to greatly appreciate those who worked in a more family-centered, collaborative way, listened actively and respected family input, and offered support based on the children's specific needs (Dunlap & Fox, 2007). Families commented on some of the very special connections they had made with those professionals who they felt really took an interest in their children and worked especially hard to partner for their success.

Transitions between programs often posed challenges for parents as they worked to find their way through the bureaucratic maze of paperwork, different rules and practices, and interactions with a whole new set of professionals. Finding someone who really understood what you needed to do to move smoothly through the process seemed like a miracle to one mother, who referred to an especially helpful facilitator as "another little angel." Another family talked about the comprehensive, family-centered hospital-based system they participated in with their children from an early age, which helped to set them on a positive path that they continued to honor in their collaborations with other new professionals in their lives.

Relationships with professionals that worked well were grounded in clear communication, honest assessments, and reciprocity (Dunlap & Fox, 2007). One family shared the ways that they made a conscious effort to personalize their interactions with the professionals working with their children, making sure that they knew from the start the things that would most make a difference for them on a daily basis. They understood that systems for keeping ongoing communication between home and school require a shared commitment to the process.

Many of the families said that professionals had provided support for them, as well as for their children. They learned from them and with them how to best meet their children's needs as a parent. One mother referenced some particularly helpful practitioners who were able to listen without judgment, simply being alongside her to help her process new information as she made important decisions for her child's future. Several of the families commented on the importance of being able to be open to hearing what professionals had to say, just as they wanted to also be heard.

The six families represented in this book have amassed a phenomenal body of knowledge and insight about caring for and parenting children with disabilities. Although each child and family's experience is unique, their advice to others can be applied flexibly to meet the needs of many other families who are raising children with special needs. Their words touch on the thoughts and feelings that many families experience (Maul & Singer, 2009), and resonate with the strengths that have guided these families on their journeys.

The families offered heartening suggestions about negotiating with schools and districts to meet their children's educational needs. They encouraged other families to be positive and constructive in their interactions without "burning bridges," while at the same time being willing to advocate for the best supports for their child. They used words like "be strong," "don't settle," and "grow a thick skin" in describing this process.

They also encouraged families to work hard, trust their judgment, and to "act boldly" in securing appropriate services for their children. They encouraged parents not to give up, to keep going, even though much of what you do for your child may not be seen or appreciated by others. As one mother put it, quoting a professional's advice, "you have to learn to clap for yourself."

The families talked about their growing capacity to celebrate small gains and adjust their expectations, and to learn to embrace and enjoy their children for who they are. Some of the families found the poem "Welcome to Holland" (Kingsley, 1987) a useful metaphor for their lives, inspiring them to be open to the unexpected journey that they are on, rather than focusing only on what they might be missing. They encouraged other families to continue to educate themselves and others about their children's disabilities and to help their children learn to understand their needs and to advocate for themselves from an early age. They shared how valuable it is to get to know other families of children with disabilities, who can be a great source of support and understanding (Ludlow et al., 2012).

Families also had a lot to say to professionals about what they believe is most important for them to know. Many of the families talked about the need for professionals to demonstrate patience, kindness, and understanding. Some parents felt that professionals should also be loving toward their children. It was particularly important that professionals focus on the positive, emphasize what the children can do, and not underestimate their potential. Some families felt that passion for the work was also essential for professionals working with children with disabilities, while one mother suggested that those who work with the most challenging children should be paid higher salaries as an incentive to work harder and reduce turnover.

The families shared the ways that they have experienced professionals as helpful as well as unhelpful (Prezant & Marshak, 2006). Nearly all of the families underscored the critical value of knowing their children, understanding who they are and how they learn. It was especially important to some that professionals adapt their interventions to meet the individual needs of their children, rather than simply following "the textbook." For children who work with classroom assistants, one family endorsed easy, friendly, and non-intrusive support, the way a "friend" or a "golf caddy" might anticipate and provide what is needed.

Suggestions were offered for collaboration with families that respected their input (Goodley & Tregaskis, 2006), valued the role of fathers, and gave families information that draws on research. One family suggested that professionals not be afraid to reach out to parents to ask for ideas if they are finding their own strategies unsuccessful with the child. It was also noted that professionals should check in with families as often as needed to be sure that they are keeping the individual child and family in mind (Blue-Banning et al., 2004).

One mother stressed the need for professional advocacy that fosters inclusive experiences for children with disabilities (Recchia & Lee, 2013). The responsibility for creating a sense of inclusion and belonging for all children should be a collective one, that engages all members of the community and expands beyond the school walls (Maul & Singer, 2009).

When asked what they have learned about themselves through their children, the families provided very thoughtful responses (Beighton & Wills, 2017). They talked about the ways that their own emotional capacity has been strengthened, becoming richer and stronger. They see themselves as more accepting, loving, positive, compassionate, and aware. As one mother so beautifully put it, she has become "all that I want other people to be!"

The families also talked about their own capacity for patience, which they now see as greater than some of them realized, and their ability to understand children with disabilities in ways that they had never thought about before. They are grateful for small things, including each step toward progress. Some expressed surprise at how strong they have learned they are, and their ability to be "bold" and "courageous" when advocating for their children. Several talked about learning to trust their own judgment in the face of having so many professional opinions about their children.

Almost all of the families had something to say about what they now knew about the depth of their own capacity to love their children, and to fight for them to have the best possible life. For one of the families, coming to know professionals and others who gave so much of themselves in working with their children helped them to see the best in people, and to ultimately try harder to do the best for other people in their lives.

As authors, we feel privileged to have had the opportunity to participate in these family conversations. The families shared their stories with honesty, emotion, and authenticity, allowing us a glimpse into their thoughts, feelings, history, and daily life. Listening in, we came to know something about this diverse group of people who are working together to bring their own personal and shared strengths to the process of being a family. Contrary to the early literature that portrayed families of children with disabilities as living a life of tragedy (Maul & Singer, 2009), we hear from families who are strong, resilient (Bayat, 2007), and able to be optimistic about their children's future, despite some lingering fears (Slattery et al., 2017).

We learn from these families that professionals are not always helpful, and their ways of being can have long-term impacts on them and their children (Dunlap & Fox, 2007). Because families of children with disabilities often receive specialized intervention services at a young age, they must learn to negotiate with professionals from early in their children's lives. Questions about who owns the expertise (Goodley & Tregaskis, 2006) may arise as families come to their own understandings about parenting, and the very nature of how they can be at their best with their children. Families tell us that they do know their children very well; their understandings about them are rooted in their cultural contexts, and nurtured by their deep love for them. Their unique knowledge about how their children participate in daily life can and should be foundational to the family–professional partnerships that evolve (Dunlap & Fox, 2007.

Creating family–professional partnerships that really work depends on the ability to suspend judgment, listen compassionately, respect alternative ideas, come to shared understandings (Blue-Banning et al. 2004; Dunlap & Fox, 2007; Puig, Erwin, Evenson, & Beresford, 2015; Recchia & Williams, 2006), and work together to make changes happen. Although this can be challenging, the families offer some helpful strategies for both other families and professionals. Striving for this ideal in working with families remains a cornerstone not only to ensuring children's and families' rights but also to quality professional practice (IDEA, 2015).

In our own work with children, families, and teacher education students, we have come to honor and value family stories as a vehicle for developing deeper understandings of unique and diverse family contexts, the strengths that emerge within them, and the ways that children's and families' needs can best be met (Maul & Singer, 2009; Goodley & Tregaskis, 2006). In Chapter 8, we present a framework for bringing families and others as guest speakers into classes for current and future professionals who work with children with disabilities and their families.

It's important to remember that every family is on their own unique journey. Families' strengths and resilience may look different, depending on where and when professionals intersect with them along the way. It is our good fortune that the families we meet here were poised to share their experiences with us. Through their stories, they guide us to consistently nurture strong family-professional partnerships, create cohesive interdisciplinary collaboration, and engage the larger community in supporting and including children with disabilities and their families. We hope that readers will find inspiration here for seeing families' interests and motivations more clearly, and for building meaningful alliances with them in the future.

References

Barr, J., & McLeod, S. (2010). They never see how hard it is to be me: Siblings' observations of strangers, peers, and family. *International Journal of Speech-Language Pathology*, 12(2), 162–171.

Bayat, M. (2007). Evidence of resilience in families of children with autism. *Journal of Intellectual Disability Research*, 51(9), 702–714.

Beighton, C., & Wills, J. (2017). Are parents identifying positive aspects to parenting their child with an intellectual disability or are they just coping? A qualitative exploration. *Journal of Intellectual Disabilities*, 21(4), 325–345.

Blue-Banning, M., Summers, J. A., Frankland, H. C., Nelson, L. L., & Beegle, G. (2004). Dimensions of family and professional partnerships: Constructive guidelines for collaboration. *Exceptional Children*, 70(2), 167–184.

Crettenden, A., Lam, J., & Denson, L. (2018). Grandparent support of mothers caring for a child with a disability: Impacts for maternal mental health. *Research in Developmental Disabilities*, 76, 35–45.

Dunlap, G., & Fox, L. (2007). Parent-professional partnerships: A valuable context for addressing challenging behaviors. *International Journal of Disability, Development and Education*, 54(3), 273–285.

Farrugia, D. (2009). Exploring stigma: Medical knowledge and the stigmatisation of parents of children diagnosed with autism spectrum disorder. *Sociology of Health and Illness*, 31(7), 1011–1027.

González, N., Moll, L., & Amanti, C. (2005). *Funds of knowledge: Theorizing practices in households, communities and classrooms*. Mahwah, NJ: Lawrence Erlbaum.

Goodley, D., & Tregaskis, C. (2006). Storying disability and impairment: Retrospective accounts of disabled family life. *Qualitative Health Research*, 16(5), 630–646.

Individuals with Disabilities Education Act (IDEA) (P.L. 108–446) (2015). Retrieved from https://sites.ed.gov/idea/

Kingsley, E. P. (1987). Welcome to Holland. Retrieved from wwwndss.org/resources/a-parents-perspective/

Lawrence-Lightfoot, S. (2016). Portraiture methodology: Blending art and science. *LEARNing Landscapes* 9(2), 19–27.

Lee, M., & Gardener, J. E. (2010). Grandparents' involvement and support in families with children with disabilities. *Educational Gerontology*, 36(6), 467–499.

Lee, Y.-J., Park, H., & Recchia, S. L. (2016). Embracing each other and growing together: Redefining the meaning of caregiving a child with disabilities. *Journal of Child and Family Studies*, 24(12), 3662–3675.

Ludlow, A., Skelly, C., & Rohleder, P. (2012). Challenges faced by parents of children diagnosed with autism spectrum disorder. *Journal of Health Psychology*, 17(5), 702–711.

Maul, C. A., & Singer, G. H. S. (2009). "Just good different things": Specific accommodations families make to positively adapt to their children with developmental disabilities. *Topics in Early Childhood Special Education*, 29(3), 155–170.

Prezant, F. P., & Marshak, L. (2006). Helpful actions seen through the eyes of parents of children with disabilities. *Disability and Society*, 21(1), 31–45.

Puig, V. I. (2012). Cultural and linguistic alchemy: Mining the resources of Spanish-speaking children and families receiving early intervention services. *Journal of Research in Childhood Education*, 26(3), 325–345.

Puig, V. I., Erwin, E. J., Evenson, T. L., & Beresford, M. (2015). "It's a two-way street": Examining how trust, diversity, and contradiction influence a sense of community. *Journal of Research in Childhood Education*, 29(2), 187–201.

Recchia, S. L., & Lee, Y.-J. (2013). *Inclusion in the early childhood classroom: What makes a difference?* New York: Teachers College Press.

Recchia, S. L., & Williams, L. R. (2006). Culture, class, and diversity: Implications for practice. In G. Foley and J. Hochman (Eds.), *Infant mental health in early intervention: Achieving unity in principles and practice*. Baltimore, MD: Paul H. Brookes Publishing Co.

Slattery, E., McMahon, J., & Gallagher, S. (2017). Optimism and benefit finding in parents of children with developmental disabilities: The role of positive reappraisal and social support. *Research in Developmental Disabilities*, 65, 12–22.

APPENDIX

Interview Protocol

1. Tell me about yourself and your family

- Who are the members of your family?
- Who are other important people in your family's life?
- In what ways have these family members and other important people provided you with support and assistance in raising your child/ren?
- What are some things that seem to be going especially well?
- What are the major strengths of your family?

2. Tell me about your child

- What would you like other people to understand about your child(ren)?
- What are some of the particular challenges that your child(ren) is/are facing now?
- What do you feel good about as a parent?
- What have you learned about yourself through your child(ren)?
- What are some goals and dreams you have for your child(ren)?
- Can you think of ways that educators and other professionals can help you support these goals and expectations?

3. Tell me about your child's/ren's educational experiences

- Can you tell me about the process of accessing services and support?
- Can you identify guiding principles that have informed your decisions about your child(ren)'s educational settings and services?
- Please describe your child(ren) and family's experience transitioning to different educational settings.

- What other experiences have contributed to your child(ren)'s educational and social growth and development (for example, family activities or extracurricular activities)?
- Describe the communication and collaboration that takes place between professionals and your family.
- How would you like your child to look back on his/her early educational experiences?

4. Tell me about your family's daily life and community experiences

- What is a typical day in the life of your family?
- What are the most enjoyable aspects of the day?
- What are the most challenging aspects of the day?
- What is a favorite special activity that you or your family enjoys sharing?
- Are there special times that are celebrated by your family? How do you celebrate them together?
- Can you describe your child(ren)'s relationships with other family members?
- What are some special things that your child(ren) can learn from your family members and other important people in your family's life?

5. What advice do you see as most helpful to others?

- Can you think of any piece of advice that has been particularly helpful to you and your family?
- Is there any particular advice you wish you could pass along to families with children with disabilities?
- Is there any particular advice you wish you could pass along to professionals working with children with disabilities?

Is there anything else you would like to share? Thank you for participating.